THE BOOK OF CATHOLIC CUSTOMS AND TRADITIONS

THE BOOK OF CATHOLIC CUSTOMS AND TRADITIONS

~

*Ronda De Sola Chervin
and Carla Conley*

CHARIS

Servant Publications
Ann Arbor, Michigan

Charis Books is an imprint of Servant Publications especially
designed to serve Roman Catholics.

Scripture references, unless otherwise noted, are from the New
Revised Standard Version of the Bible, © 1989 by the Division
of Christian Education of the National Council of the Churches
of Christ in the United States of America, and are used by permission. All rights reserved.

Published by Servant Publications
P.O. Box 8617
Ann Arbor, Michigan 48107

Cover design by Janice Hendrick, Good Visuals

99 00 01 02 03 04 11 10 9 8 7 6

Printed in the United States of America
ISBN 0-89283-796-9

Library of Congress Cataloging-in-Publication Data

Chervin, Ronda.
  The book of Catholic customs and traditions / Ronda De Sola
Chervin and Carla Conley.
      p.   cm.
  Includes index.
  ISBN 0-89283-796-9
  1. Catholic Church—Customs and practices.   2. Family—
Religious life.   I. Conley, Carla.   II. Title.
BX2350.2.C4946 1994
249'.08'822—dc20   94-33698
                                                                              CIP

CONTENTS

Introduction

JULIE, A YOUNG MOTHER WE KNOW, told us of driving to the market during one Advent season and seeing a billboard that proclaimed, "Keep Christ in Christmas."

"Great!" she exclaimed. "Of course I want my children to love the mystery of Christmas! But what is the best way to get the message across?"

Julie's mother had told her of how *her* mother used to set up a nativity scene in the living room long before Christmas, and bake delicious cookies almost every night in December. The family would often gather around the nativity scene in the evening and sing Christmas hymns and traditional carols.

"But my mom was a 'career mom,' and had no time for all these customs," Julie observed. "I wish I could find a book full of ideas for all the seasons and feast days of the Church to supplement the services at my parish."

Perhaps you feel the same way as Julie. Or perhaps you can identify with our experiences, which led us to write *The Book of Catholic Customs and Traditions.*

When I first became a Catholic in 1959, at the age of

twenty-one, what drew me most to the Church was the joy of finding truth, absolute truth, in the form of a person, Jesus Christ, present to me in the sacraments. But these lofty realities were buttressed by all the little customs and traditions I observed among the Catholics who brought me into the faith: holy water fonts inside the doors of their homes, flowers brought on the feast day of a person's patron saint, scapulars around the necks of little children (and some adults too).

When I became a mother the most important thing to me was to give my children a sense of the beauty and greatness of being Catholic. Praying aloud, bringing them to Mass, and telling them about Jesus, Mary, and the saints were the main ways I introduced them to the life of faith. But I soon found that home traditions were important too, making religion more cozy and personal for them—and for me as well. Carla Conley, my co-author, is one of my daughters who enjoyed these customs and is now passing them on to her own children.

In many Catholic homes, however, the observance of these customs and traditions declined after Vatican II. This may have been a side effect of an effort to focus on the loving Jesus as the center of our faith; practices that could seem to pull the heart away from that focus were put aside.

Now it should be easier for every Catholic to find Jesus as his or her personal Savior. Perhaps, then, it is time to reintroduce some of the old devotions and customs—not as substitutes for love of Jesus but as a way to experience the richness of grace in the many forms the Holy Spirit has inspired the Church to provide for us.

Our *Book of Catholic Customs and Traditions* is designed to help not only parents but all Catholics to enjoy ways of celebrating God's love day by day through-out the liturgical year. The first chapter offers suggestions for encouraging daily family devotions; like most of the practices in this book, these can be adapted for use by single people with their friends or in Christian communi-ties. Other chapters focus on specific liturgical seasons: Advent, Christmas, Lent, Easter, and also Ordinary Time. Chapter seven presents a variety of customs and practices that can be used at any time of the year.

Throughout the book we have given background information for lesser known customs and traditions. We have also tried to include a number of customs and recipes from other countries, with a view to communicat-ing something of the richness of traditions outside our own culture. An index at the back will help you find any particular customs you are looking for.

As we have worked on this book, Carla and I have come to an even deeper appreciation of the richness of our Catholic heritage. We offer you this fruit of our labor and of our family experience, and we pray:

May God bless all of us as we pass down the traditions of the past to new generations of Catholics. We ask you, Mother Mary, to intercede for us so that our times of preparation and of ceremony may be filled with peace rather than fuss and frustration. Through the customs and traditions in this book may our families and friends be brought to greater love for you, dear Jesus, for each other, and for every part of the creation of our loving God.

Ronda De Sola Chervin

Ronda De Sola Chervin

CHAPTER 1

~

FAMILY DEVOTIONS
A Place to Find God Daily

PRAYING TOGETHER IS AN IMPORTANT and time-honored practice in Catholic families—one that establishes a foundation for celebrating the customs and traditions of the liturgical year. Here are a few suggestions for making such devotions a part of the daily life of your family or community group.

It is a good idea to set up a devotional area or prayer nook in the dining room, living room, kitchen, or parental bedroom where you can join together for prayer. Among the items you can put in such a place are:

- the Bible
- statues with vigil lights
- pictures of Jesus, Mary, Joseph, and other saints
- a church calendar
- rosaries
- a holy water font
- a book of the Liturgy of the Hours
- other holy objects of your choice

Family devotions, which typically take place before bedtime, may include any number of customs that your family finds meaningful: singing a favorite song, praying a rosary together (adding special intentions), reading a passage from Scripture, blessing one another with holy water or oil, exchanging a sign of peace.

This need not be a rigid routine. You may wish to change and supplement these prayers and practices to fit particular liturgical seasons and feast days. This book describes many customs and traditions that could be incorporated into your times of family prayer.

It may take some effort to establish a regular pattern for family devotions, but it is worth persisting because the benefits are many. Parents who lead their families in daily prayer teach by their example the importance of knowing Jesus in a personal way. Family prayer times provide the foundation that children need to grow to Christian maturity, teaching them to love the Lord Jesus and follow his commandments every day of their lives, not just on Sundays.

Family devotions provide a time for reading Bible stories and stories of the saints. These will enrich your family's faith and provide positive role models for children and adults alike.

Family prayer times teach children to be sensitive to the needs of other people, and encourage a willingness to help others in times of need. Some families use this time to build unity through reconciliation—to ask and receive forgiveness for offenses committed against other family members during the day.

Also, from this devotional center will flow many other ways of creating a holy atmosphere in your home. For example, you might play Christian classical or popular music throughout the day or at special hours. Such practices convey to everyone in the household—members as well as visitors—that the most important person in your family is Jesus Christ.

Another simple way to encourage an awareness of God in your home is to make use of the opportunities that arise in ordinary conversation. Little phrases that turn the mind to the way of the Lord Jesus can be a great help to growth in holiness. You might try sprinkling some of these into your everyday conversations:

God bless you (as a departing salutation or on the phone or inserted at the end of voice mail messages).

We got the check, *praise the Lord!*

I'll see you tomorrow, *God willing.*

An Irish custom is to proclaim "In the name of God" on one's way out the door. Slovak Catholics greet anyone entering their homes—and even their schools or stores—with the words *"Pochvalen bud Pan Jezis Kristus,"* answered by *"Na veky, Amen."* This means "the Lord Jesus Christ be with you"—"and also with you."

Although thoughtless, constant repetition of such phrases can make them seem trite or meaningless, their use in moderation bespeaks a Catholic consciousness and has a certain witness value as well.

Of course, neither the family prayer time nor this result—a more spiritual atmosphere in the home—is an exclusively Catholic ideal. These are basics of Christian family life. But as we strengthen this foundation, we will be able to celebrate our Catholic customs and traditions in a richer, more meaningful way.

CHAPTER 2
~

THE ADVENT SEASON

First Sunday of Advent through Christmas Eve

The season of Advent (from the Latin "to come") begins on the Sunday nearest to November 30 and is the first season in the liturgical year. Advent is a time of preparation, anticipating the celebration of the birth of Christ on Christmas Day—and of Jesus' second coming as well.

To make the most of Advent, try to set aside some time before this busy season begins. Pray about the deeper meaning of Advent and reflect: why do we wait in joyful hope for the coming of our Lord?

~ Traditions for the Entire Season ~

Advent Angels (Christkind). Each member of your family can become an "Advent Angel" who does special things (usually in secret) for another family member. Write the name of each member on a piece of paper and put it in a hat or dish. Then have everyone draw a name to determine whose Advent Angel they will be. Explain that angels should concentrate on their charges, thinking of many little ways to show them that they are loved. This custom is also known as adopting a *Christkind*. Here the family member whose name is drawn represents a little Christ child to take care of.

Advent calendar. Children like to use an Advent calendar to mark the days before Christmas. These calendars feature twenty-four little windows, and each day one is opened to reveal a picture appropriate to the season. Some calendars include references to biblical passages; parents and children can look these up and read them together every day to make this a family ceremony.

You can buy an Advent calendar at any religious goods store. Or make one yourself by drawing or pasting religious pictures on a piece of cardboard and covering it with another piece of cardboard in which you have cut fold-up windows with numbers. Remember that the last window should display a large picture of the baby Jesus.

Advent wreath. To focus your family on Christ's coming, place an Advent wreath in a prominent spot in your home. These can be purchased in a variety of materials, including wood and metal. You can also make your own out of evergreen boughs, which symbolize immortality. Normally, Advent wreaths are circular (symbolic of eternity) or triangular (symbolic of the Trinity). Some are decorated with purple ribbons—purple is the color of Advent.

Each wreath holds three purple candles and one pink one. These are lit beginning on the first Sunday of Advent: one purple candle for the first week, two on the second Sunday and for the week following, and so on. The pink candle is lit (along with two purple candles) on the third Sunday of Advent, called "Joyful Sunday" because it provides a refreshing break from the penitential aspects of the season. Some people add a white candle, to be lit on Christmas Eve. Simple prayers and hymns can accompany the lighting of the candles, making this a daily ceremony for the whole family.

Placing a wreath (without the candles!) on the door is another Advent custom. The wreath should be made of or include holly because its thorny leaves and red berries are symbolic of the crown of thorns and drops of blood on the Savior's head.

Christmas balls. Young children can prepare gifts for other family members by adapting a German custom of giving balls with little presents inside. You will need yarn as well as tiny, inexpensive items. Go to the store with your children and select such gifts. Then work with your children to wrap the items in yarn, tying them in when possible.

Christmas cards. Most Catholics send cards with a religious message. You can buy these cards or make them yourself—a good project for your children. As your family receives cards, you and your children can create a collage or a mobile to display them.

Christmas cookies. This is a favorite tradition in many homes all over the world! Usually, Christmas baking begins during the week before Christmas. We have included some recipes at the end of this chapter, or you can make your own favorites.

Christmas tree decorating. Decorating a tree at Christmas is especially meaningful for Christians. Trees have so much symbolic meaning for us—going all the way back to the Tree of Life in the Garden of Eden. Christ too is viewed as the Tree of Life, and it was on the tree of the cross that he won life for us.

Many Catholics have a tradition of saying a blessing for the Christmas tree after it is decorated. You can have members of your family or group take turns making up blessings, or use ours:

Blessing for a Christmas Tree

Lord God, bless our tree,
Which stands alone and gleaming,
Green eternal, lighted by our hopes and
  ornamented by round dreams where we hold you,
Ropes of days and deeds on which we climb up,
To the star of promise we can but imagine
  in our tinsel and our paper gleams, reaching up to you
God bless our tree.

Crèche (Nativity scene, Christmas crib). The crèche is a representation of the manger and setting in which Christ was born. The first crèche was set up by St. Francis of Assisi, who used actual people and animals. Later, people used life-size figures of clay. Nowadays, it is most common to use tiny figures of clay, plastic, or wood.

Some crèches are very elaborate. In Italy, birthplace of the crèche, for example, there are many elaborate customs involving nativity scenes. Each church assembles a huge display, often depicting an entire town, to represent Bethlehem. There are thousands of pieces, including such droll items as tiny chamber pots under the beds! During the Advent season, it is the custom of Italians to go from church to church with the family, visiting these works of art.

Other crèches are quite simple, constructed of figures made by children with modeling clay. You can buy a crèche or make one, adding your own creative touches. In Germany, people line the bottom of the crèche with straw or cotton. One German family we knew made their crèche with rock so it looked like a cave.

Some families invest in larger—sometimes life-sized—nativity sets of plaster or wooden statues of Mary, Joseph, the infant Jesus and other characters, human and animal. They arrange these figures prominently on the front lawn, sometimes adding lights. Some families create little ceremonies for setting up the crèche: they may add one piece to the scene every night, or they may bring the three kings closer to the crèche as Epiphany approaches. In still other families the youngest child places the Christ child in the crèche on Christmas Eve.

The Jesse tree. This custom celebrates Jesus' family tree. In the Old Testament, Jesse was the father of David and lived in Bethlehem. Jesus is a descendant of Jesse, as this prophecy from the Book of Isaiah indicates: "A shoot shall come out from the stump of Jesse, and a branch shall grow out of his roots" (Is 11:1).

A Jesse tree depicts this family tree, using symbols to represent some of the characters in Jesus' lineage:

Jesse, David, Solomon, Joseph and Mary, Jesus. Or the family can begin before Jesse: Adam, Noah, Abraham, Joseph, Isaac, Jacob, Moses, Jesse.

To make your own Jesse tree, chose symbols to represent some or all of these ancestors of Jesus. Create a hanging ornament for each symbol: a rainbow for Noah, perhaps, or a harp for David, or a flowering branch for Jesse.

Start your tree by putting a bare branch in a pot and hanging the symbol for Jesse. Depending on how many ancestors you have chosen, you can hang one or two or more symbols each week of Advent. As you decorate the Jesse tree with your family or group, you might try reading a Bible story about the person whose ornament is hung on the tree that night.

Poor child decorations. Almsgiving is a common practice among many Catholics during Advent as well as Lent. Here is one lovely custom that can encourage children to give to the poor during Advent. Create some Christmas tree decorations of little boys and girls. These can be little dolls or simple paper cutouts. On each one write the name of a child from a needy family. Then have each child in your family select one of these figures. During Advent your child can pray for this other child and also buy a small gift for him or her.

"O" antiphons. One week before Christmas, in special preparation for the feast, many Catholics begin praying short prayers called the "O" antiphons. These recall some of the titles of Jesus, and there is one for every day before Christmas Eve. You and your family or group can read or chant these antiphons, which were

taken from the Liturgy of the Hours, in unison around your Advent wreath or in your special devotional area.

December 17: "O Wisdom, O Holy Word of God, you govern all creation with your strong and tender care. Come and show your people the way to salvation."

December 18: "O Sacred Lord of Ancient Israel, who showed yourself to Moses in the burning bush, who gave him the holy law on Sinai Mountain: Come, stretch out your mighty hand to set us free."

December 19: "O Flower of Jesse's stem, you have been raised up as a sign for all peoples; kings stand silent in your presence; the nations bow down in worship before you. Come, let nothing keep you from coming to our aid."

December 20: "O Key of David, O Royal Power of Israel controlling at your will the gate of heaven: come break down the prison walls of death for those who dwell in darkness and the shadow of death; and lead your captive people into freedom."

December 21: "O Radiant Dawn, splendor of eternal light, sun of justice: come, shine on those who dwell in darkness and the shadow of death."

December 22: "O King of all the nations, the only joy of every human heart; O Keystone of the mighty arch of man, come and save the creature you fashioned from the dust."

December 23: "O Emmanuel, king and lawgiver, desire of the nations, Savior of all people, come and set us free, Lord our God."

You can write the antiphons on separate cards with pictures to illustrate each one. Place the cards in a bowl and let each member of your family select one, passing the bowl around twice if necessary. Whoever has the antiphon for the particular day reads it during your group's time of prayer.

Posada. The *posada* is a Mexican tradition that commemorates Mary and Joseph's arrival in Bethlehem and their search for a place to sleep somewhere in the city. The outcome is well-known: a local innkeeper takes pity on them and allows the couple to sleep in his stable, which is where Jesus is born. (You will find the story in Luke 2:7-20.)

You can organize a *posada* with three or four other families or groups. Here is how it works. One family goes to the second family's house and asks to be let in—like Mary and Joseph in Bethlehem—but are told that there is no room. Both families then proceed to the third family's house and the process is repeated. When all families arrive at the last house, they knock on the door and ask several times to come in. At last they are let inside, and everyone sings carols and eats Christmas treats.

Sometimes the parish organizes the *posada*. A group of parishioners holding candles walks to several houses, knocking on their closed doors. They end up at the church, where they are invited in for prayers and singing. This custom has been adopted in other countries as well.

∼ *Special Days of the Season* ∼

St. Barbara ....December 4
St. Nicholas.................................December 6
Feast of the Immaculate
    Conception...............................December 8
Our Lady of Guadalupe ....December 12
St. Lucy ....December 13

∼ *For Your Home* ∼

Make a joyful noise... Sing Christmas carols around the wreath every Sunday and serve loads of cookies afterwards!

Let the kids make an Advent wreath! The wreath below is fun for children to make even if you can afford to buy the more expensive kind. Be sure to remind them to light the candles only when an adult is present.

    You will need:
- a large piece of cardboard
- half an egg carton
- four candles
- green material such as leaves, paper, pine needles, or even grass
- glue and scissors

    Cut a large donut shape out of the cardboard. Cut four "cups" out of the egg carton, one for each candle, and glue them onto the cardboard wreath. Glue on the green material around the cups.

Plant St. Lucy's wheat. A lovely Hungarian custom is to plant wheat on St. Lucy's Day, December 13. It will sprout and grow green, ready for offering to the baby Jesus on Christmas Day. You can involve your children in this custom by creating a wheat-planting ceremony. Spread the seeds on top of the soil in a small flowerpot and push them gently into the earth, but not too deep. Water the wheat daily, and offer the result to Jesus by placing the pot in front of the manger on Christmas Day. (For more information on St. Lucy, see the feast day section of chapter six.)

Do good deeds to warm the baby Jesus. At the beginning of Advent, lay out strings of yarn near the crèche. Anyone who does a good deed takes a piece of yarn and puts it on top of the crèche. At the end of Advent, braid the strings together and sew the braids into a rug to line the crèche.

Make St. Nicholas cookies (Speculatius). Behind Santa Claus stands a real person: St. Nicholas, a saintly bishop of the fourth century. In Holland, Belgium, and other countries, these cookies, pressed or cut out in the shape of a bishop, are served on St. Nicholas Day, December 6.

This is a good opportunity to tell your children about this saint of God, the *real* Santa Claus. St. Nicholas was known for his kindness to those in distress, so you might use his story to emphasize the importance of caring for poor people. You might also suggest doing something as a family to help the poor—work in a soup kitchen, take food or Christmas treats to a needy family. (For more information on St. Nicholas, see the feast days section of chapter six.)

ST. NICHOLAS COOKIES

1 cup butter
1 cup shortening
2 cups brown sugar
1/2 teaspoon baking soda
4 teaspoons cinnamon
1/2 teaspoon nutmeg
1/2 teaspoon cloves
4-1/2 cups flour
1/2 cup sour cream
1/2 cup chopped nuts

Cream butter and shortening with brown sugar. Sift dry ingredients together and add alternately with sour cream. Stir in nuts. Dough should be firm enough to roll into wax paper. Chill for at least an hour, but preferably overnight. When dough is chilled, roll out and cut out the bishop shapes, using a stencil cut from light cardboard. Bake at 350° F for approximately 12 minutes. Cool and decorate as desired.

Bake Christmas cookies! Make your favorite recipes for holiday treats and for giving to friends and family. Or use some of our family's favorite cookie recipes:

LEBKUCHEN

4 eggs	1 teaspoon cinnamon
2 cups brown sugar	2 ounces citron, cut fine
2 cups flour	1/4 pound almonds or pecans

Beat eggs and sugar until fluffy. Mix flour and cinnamon with finely chopped nuts and citron; combine the two mixtures. Spread dough in two greased 10 x 15-inch pans. Bake at 375° F for 25 minutes. Cool, cut into bars and frost with plain icing.

NUT BUSSERLN

1 egg, beaten	1 cup chopped walnuts
1 cup sugar	5 tablespoons flour

Beat egg and sugar until very light; stir in chopped nuts, then add flour. Drop by teaspoonfuls on greased cookie sheet and bake at 375° F about 10 minutes. Cool on waxed paper.

RUM BALLS

1/2 pound vanilla wafers	1/2 cup light corn syrup
2 teaspoons cocoa	1/4 cup rum or brandy
1 cup pecans, chopped fine	confectioner's sugar

Grind wafers very fine. Add nuts, cocoa, syrup, and rum. Stir until well blended. Dust hands with confectioner's sugar and roll mixture into balls the size of a walnut. Let stand for about an hour to dry partially. Then roll in confectioner's sugar. Dry completely on waxed paper.

PFEFFERNUSSE

2 cups corn syrup	1 teaspoon baking soda
2 cups dark molasses	2 teaspoons cinnamon
1 cup shortening	1/4 pound citron, cut fine
1 lemon, rind and juice	1/4 pound almonds, chopped fine
1 cup brown sugar	confectioner's sugar
10 cups flour	

Warm syrup and molasses, add shortening and lemon juice and remaining ingredients in order given, soda mixed with flour. Roll into little balls and brush with egg white. Place on greased pan a few inches apart. Bake at 350° F until brown. Roll in confectioner's sugar.

CHAPTER 3

〜

THE CHRISTMAS SEASON

Christmas Eve through the Feast
of the Baptism of the Lord

The name "Christmas" comes from the words "Christ" and "mass." The celebration of Christmas was introduced around the fourth century, perhaps as a counter-celebration to the pagan festivities surrounding the winter solstice, when the longest night of the year occurs. Although Scripture does not tell us that Jesus was born on December 25, it seems fitting that we celebrate God's greatest gift during the time of our greatest darkness here on earth.

Some Catholics get caught up with the gift buying, holiday party preparation, and general "busyness" of the season. Others are so intent not to let commercialism take over Christmas that they lose sight of the joy of sharing with others, and they too lose the real meaning of the season.

We recommend that you spend some time meditating on the coming of the light of Christ into our world of darkness. Think about what this feast must have signified to the Christians who first celebrated it, and try to align your spirit with theirs.

∼ *Traditions for the Season of Christmas* ∼

Austrian Christmas. In Austria, it is customary to have Christmas punch and *stollen,* a special bread, after midnight Mass. (Both of these recipes can be found at the end of this chapter.)

Christ candle. Some people light a large candle, symbolizing the coming of Jesus, to burn throughout the night of Christmas Eve.

Christkind letters. Another special Austrian custom is to write a letter to the *Christkind,* the Christ child. Written by adults and children alike, these letters contain resolutions as well as wishes for gifts. They are said to be delivered to the Christ child by the writers' guardian angels! This is a lovely way to adapt the traditional letter to Santa Claus.

Christmas presents. Christmas is often the time for giving presents as an expression of love. In some families each member selects or makes gifts for everyone in the family. In other families, especially larger ones with grown children, members "draw names." This way, everyone receives only one gift and buys only one gift, for the person whose name was drawn. This cuts down on expense and de-emphasizes the material aspects of Christmas.

Still other families decide not to give family gifts at

all. Instead, they use the money to buy gifts for the needy or to make some other charitable donation.

Christmas meal. On Christmas Day it is traditional to have a special dinner with as many family members as possible present. If there are disputes about who should get to host the meal, one solution if family members live in the same area is to have two celebrations. The younger members of the family can go to the home of one set of grandparents or in-laws on Christmas Eve and have another festive gathering on Christmas Day. If family members live far away from each other, families can take turns hosting the celebration on alternate years.

Filipino Christmas. In the Philippines, Christmas is anticipated with *Simbang Gabi*, a celebration that begins on December 16. This custom originated from a tradition of offering Masses in honor of Our Lady of Advent for the nine days before Christmas—a novena of Masses.

On these nine days before Christmas the *misa de gallo*, or "Masses of the cock," take place before dawn. Bands go through the streets and church bells ring to call the people out to worship. Inside the church there are brilliant lights, plants, lanterns, and streamers. The altar is decorated with a scene of Bethlehem.

After Mass the early birds partake of rice cakes and tea offered by groups of women outside the church. The boys offer treats to the girls, who politely refuse, laughing among themselves. In my (Ronda's) parish in Los Angeles, Filipinos still celebrate *Simbang Gabi*, but more simply—in the evening, with streamers decorating the church.

After Christmas Eve dinner in the Philippines, there is a pageant depicting Mary and Joseph's search for shelter. Statues of the holy couple are carried through the streets in procession; they stop at designated houses but are turned away. Finally, the procession reaches the church and everyone is received inside.

At midnight Mass, the figure of the infant Jesus is added to the nativity scene. To mark this, a lantern in the form of a comet has been strung above the congregation. Representing the star of Bethlehem, it moves from the choir loft to the altar and stops above the baby. The children love to watch this star!

Midnight Mass is followed by a festive time of eating and drinking, song and dance. Christmas Day is devoted to the children. They are dressed well and visit their relatives and godparents. They kiss the hand of each relative and then receive treats and a little money and other gifts.

German Christmas Eve. In Germany, Christmas Eve begins in the late afternoon. The family gathers to decorate the Christmas tree, adding real candles, which are lit after all the other ornaments have been hung. Early in the evening there is music around the tree and a nativity play is performed by members of the family. After presents are exchanged, the family dines together and then the children retire, to be awakened in time for midnight Mass.

Happy Birthday, Jesus. Some people with young children have a birthday party for Jesus on Christmas Eve or Christmas Day. You can make a small birthday cake or cupcakes for this. If you have a wooden figure of the baby Jesus, try baking it into the cake. Whoever finds it can take it to the Christmas crib while all sing "Happy Birthday."

Midnight Mass. Most churches celebrate a special midnight Mass on Christmas Eve. Many families like to attend this liturgy and plan ahead by giving their young children a nap early in the day. Some people go to confession just before the Christmas Eve Mass begins.

A Nativity play. Families or groups might want to write and prepare a simple nativity play to perform on Christmas Eve.

This project can involve everyone; those who don't want to act in the play can make costumes and scenery.

Polish Oplatek—The blessed Christmas wafer. In Poland, families celebrate Christmas Eve by partaking of a special Christmas wafer. These wafers, often made in convents, are stamped with a picture of the Nativity. In a solemn ceremony, reminding all of the One who is being awaited, the head of the family takes the wafer and breaks off a piece; the wafer is then passed on to the other members, each one breaking off a piece. The ceremony takes place as part of a meal, and there is an extra place set for Christ. If you wish to follow this custom, you can adapt it by using homemade bread or rolls or even crackers.

A Slovak Christmas. This lovely account of a Slovak Christmas was written by Rosemary Yuhas James, who has allowed us to use it here:

Hand-made ornaments were always an important part of our Slovak Christmas. Many of the ornaments were made from tin foil, straw, beads, eggshells, nutshells, brocades, laces, braids, ribbons, and scraps of material—items that were easily obtainable and inexpensive.

Making ornaments is a rich tradition, bringing together families and friends to create keepsakes which have symbolism and meaning.

The *hviezda* (pronounced vee-ez-dah), or star, was the ornament used most frequently. It was made of straw, feathers, wood or whatever creativeness would allow. It reminded us of that special sign that led the three kings to the baby Jesus.

Eggshells have always been appropriate as Christmas decorations since the egg symbolizes the miracle of birth.

Birds were frequently used as ornaments: the white dove symbolizes peace. The most popular bird in Slavic decorations is the rooster, typifying health, fertility and good luck. His body was made from a blown egg. (To make a blown egg, take a fresh, uncooked egg, make quarter inch holes in both ends with a pin. Placing your lips over one end, blow the raw egg out the other hole into a dish. Wash the egg, and let it dry.)

On Christmas Eve children singing Christmas carols carried a homemade star from home to home, calling to mind the Star of Bethlehem that led the three kings to the manger.

Christmas Eve at the Yuhas home brought many relatives to celebrate. The evening was graced with the traditional Christmas Eve supper, the *Villia* supper (pronounced Vee-lee-ah, from the Latin word *vigilare*, meaning to watch). Traditionally, the *Villia* supper did not start until the first star appeared in the heavens.

The table was set with a small amount of clean straw, reminding the family that the Christ child was bedded upon straw in the manger. Our parents came to the table with a lighted candle, holy water, and honey to greet the family. There was always an empty place, which symbolized the coming of Jesus. Our mom sprinkled holy water on the table, asking God to bless the food to be eaten. Dad took a bit of honey and made the sign of the cross on the foreheads of all present. This was to remind us to be pleasant and that we might sweeten our lives.

The meal began with the *oplatky* (pronounced oh-plaht-kee), or "Christmas wafers." (The word *oplatky* comes from the Latin word *oblata*, which means offerings.) This is the unleavened bread with a Christmas scene on it and probably one of the most popular customs we keep in America. These were eaten with honey and shared with one another—a piece was also sent to absent family members and friends, who would partake of it at the same time as their loved ones at home.

The meal itself was carefully planned so that it contained all of nature's elements that produce foods except the fat and meat of animals, which were to be considered like humans on this day. From the forest came the mushrooms, nuts, honey and wild berries; the fields, orchards, and gardens yielded grains, cereals, fruits and vegetables. The different foods played an important part in the Christmas Eve supper.

The meal began with a bean and potato soup. Fish was the main entree since Christmas Eve was a strict day for abstaining from meat. Other foods were rice, *bobalky* (walnut-sized biscuits that were broken apart and combined in a bowl with a mixture of ground poppyseed and honey), *pirohy,* peas, mushrooms, sauerkraut, *kolache* (a Slovak pastry made with poppyseed, nuts, or pineapple-raisin filling), wine, fruit, and nuts. Everyone at the table was expected to have at least a small taste of each food served. This symbolized all the meals that would be enjoyed in the coming year.

After the *Villia* supper was over, the Christmas tree, with scenes of the nativity prominently displayed underneath, was lighted for the first time. All gathered around the piano and sang Christmas carols, many of them in Slovak. The festivities continued until it was time to leave for Midnight Mass, also known as the *pastier,* or shepherd's, Mass.

The bells of the church could be heard for miles around calling the worshipers to this great celebration. Caroling continued in the church until it was time for the Mass to begin. The procession at the start of the service included children dressed as Mary carrying the baby Jesus, Joseph, many angels and shepherds. The children processed to the front of the church where the manger was blessed by the priest in a traditional celebration. The priest then continued on with the great Mass which concluded in the wee hours of the morning with more caroling. Christmas Day always started with Mass and continued with many visitors, gifts, games and much merriment.

Wooden shoes. On Christmas Eve in Holland and other countries, wooden shoes are put outside the windowsill or door. Parents fill them with goodies.

∼ *Traditions for the Feast of Epiphany* ∼

Epiphany means "manifestation." The feast of Epiphany celebrates the revelation of the Christ child to the three kings who journeyed to Bethlehem in search of him.

In quite a number of countries, gifts are exchanged on the feast of Epiphany, rather than Christmas. Sometimes each family member is given one small gift at Christmas, and many more on Epiphany—a commemoration of the gifts of the Magi to the Christ child.

A Belgian Epiphany. Belgian children go door-to-door, dressed as the three kings, singing and receiving treats.

The chalk ceremony. One interesting custom for Epiphany is to ask God's blessing on your house by marking this inscription over your doors with chalk that has been blessed:

19 + CMB + 94

The numbers stand for the year in which the blessing is inscribed (1994, in the example above). The letters "CMB" stand for the names traditionally given to the Magi who found the Christ child—Caspar, Melchior, and Balthasar. They are also an abbreviation for the Latin blessing, *Christus mansionem benedicat,* or "Christ bless this dwelling."[1]

The chalk is blessed by a priest at church and then given out. If your church does not distribute blessed chalk, a member of your group or family can lead the following ceremony in your home:

Blessing of Chalk

Leader: Our help is in the name of the Lord.

All: Who made heaven and earth.

Leader: The Lord be with you.

All: And with your spirit.

Leader: Bless, O Lord God, this creature chalk to render it helpful to men. Grant that they who use it in faith and with it inscribe upon the entrance of their homes the names of thy saints, Caspar, Melchior, and Balthasar, may through their merits and intercession enjoy health of body and protection of soul. Through Christ our Lord, Amen.

The leader sprinkles the chalk with holy water and then sprinkles holy water over every room in the house. Finally the leader makes the inscription over every door that leads to the outside.

A Mexican Epiphany. On the evening before the feast of Epiphany, children leave their shoes outside the door or on the patio. If they have been bad, they find coals in their shoes the next day. If they have been good, they will find small gifts inside their shoes.

On the feast day itself a special large fruitcake in the shape of a donut is eaten. These cakes are given as presents on Christmas Day and have surprises baked in. Presumably, bad children find a white lima bean and the best child finds a figure of the baby Jesus. Whoever gets the baby Jesus is supposed to throw a party for the others on February 2. (A similar fruitcake is eaten on Epiphany in South American countries and in Italy.)

∽ *Traditions for the Feast of* ∽ *the Holy Innocents*

On the feast of the Holy Innocents, December 28, we honor the little children who were murdered by Herod in his attempt to kill Jesus, whom he feared would replace him as king. (See Matthew 2:1-18.)

Pro-life intercession. It is customary in some American cities to pray especially on this day for babies destroyed by abortion and to make reparation by processions and special Masses.

Litany for the unborn child. Here is a litany that many people pray on this day. Written by George Peate, it highlights the real existence of the unborn child in the womb and is titled "Litany of the Unborn Christ Child." (For information about the custom of praying litanies, see chapter seven.)[2]

Our Father, Author of life,
Thank you for the gift of life.

Word of God, through whom all things were made,
Thank you for the gift of life.

Jesus, your coming was announced by an angel,
bless the unborn and their parents.
Jesus, conceived in love by God's Spirit and
the Virgin Mary,
Jesus, beloved son of a humble carpenter,
Jesus, source of immeasurable joy for Mary and Joseph,
Jesus, the aging Elizabeth rejoiced in your presence,
Jesus, you filled the unborn Baptist with gladness,
Jesus, Mary's soul mirrors this gift of Divinity,

Jesus, because of you all generations call Mary blessed,

Jesus, one month in the womb and your tiny heart beat for love,

Jesus, another month passed and your mouth and hands were wonderfully formed,

Jesus, your mouth would tell the glory of God,

Jesus, those hands were fashioned to be pierced for love,

Jesus, before birth you rested near your mother's faithful heart,

Jesus, grateful to those who assisted your mother during pregnancy,

Jesus, teaching us: whatever we do to the least of your brothers and sisters, we do to you,

Jesus, your birth was a joyful revelation to humanity,

Jesus, days after that nativity, a fearful king planned to kill you,

Jesus, countless infants were slaughtered in your place.

Lord, thank You for first coming among us as the unborn Christ child. Today, untold numbers of our tiny sisters and brothers have been abandoned by the world's leaders, by the traditional defenders of justice, by the healing professions and even by their own parents. But you are their Savior—you have not forgotten them. Savior, rescue and protect these little ones from the neglect and violence of an uncaring world.

Merciful Lord, your tiny infant heart, which was later emptied on the cross, offers this world its only hope. Forgive us our sins against the unborn, against their parents, and against all your children. Lord, have mercy on us. Christ, have mercy on us. Lord, have mercy on us.

Prince of Peace, through your healing Spirit, help us to lovingly accept every conceived child created in your image and likeness, as a messenger of peace and goodwill toward all people. Amen.

Remembering the unborn. Many pro-life Catholics wear a "Precious Feet" pin. This shows two tiny feet the size of an unborn baby's at ten weeks, a common time for an abortion.

Some parishes have developed special traditions to commemorate the unborn on the feast of Epiphany or on January 22, the anniversary of the U.S. Supreme Court decision which legalized abortion, Roe vs. Wade. They might celebrate a memorial Mass at a cemetery and say special prayers for the victims of abortion.

∽ *Special Days of the Season* ∽

St. John the Evangelist...............December 27
Feast of the Holy Family............December 29
Solemnity of Mary,
    the Mother of God ....January 1
Feast of the Holy Name of Jesus ......January 4

∽ *For Your Home* ∽

Make your Christmas joy last as long as possible! The Church's celebration of Christmas lasts until Epiphany, so keep your decorations up, including the crib.

Happy Birthday, Jesus. When some families open their gifts, the youngest child presents the first one to the baby Jesus in the crèche. The gift is later donated to a homeless shelter or a less fortunate local family.

Tired of traditional Christmas carols? Play Handel's *Messiah* on Christmas Eve and throughout the season.

Have the Magi come to your crèche. If you don't have statues of them, find their pictures on Christmas cards, cut them out, and mount them. Or you can have members of your family or group create costumes and act out the story. (One way to do this is to bake a cake with three beans in it. Whoever gets a piece with a bean must dress up as one of the Magi and perform in the play.)

Try these recipes for an Austrian Christmas Eve!

CHRISTMAS PUNCH

1 pint water	
1 cinnamon stick, broken	juice of 4 lemons
1 vanilla bean	juice of 4 oranges
2 1/2 cups sugar	grated rind of 1 lemon
1 pineapple, sliced	grated rind of 1 orange
4 oranges, cut in pieces	1 bottle of claret
1/2 cup maraschino	1 bottle of red table wine
cherries	1/2 bottle of rum

Boil spices with the water. Remove spices and pour water into large earthenware pot. Combine fruit and sugar in a separate dish. Add fruit, lemon and orange juices and rind to the warming pot. Add wines and rum, cover and heat. Add champagne before serving, if desired.

CHRISTMAS PUNCH FOR CHILDREN

2 quarts water	juice and grated rind of 2 lemons
2 cups sugar	juice and grated rind of 2 oranges
1 cinnamon stick	1 quart grape juice
1/2 teaspoon whole cloves	

Boil water, sugar, rinds, and spices until flavored. Add grape juice, lemon juice, and orange juice. Boil five minutes, remove cloves and cinnamon, and serve hot in punch glasses.

STOLLEN

2 cakes of compressed yeast	grated rind of 1 lemon
or 2 packages of dry	1/4 cup rum
granular yeast	1 teaspoon salt
2 cups lukewarm milk	1/2 teaspoon nutmeg
4 cups flour	3/4 pound raisins
1 pound butter, softened	1/2 cup orange peel, cut fine
1 cup sugar	1/2 cup citron, cut fine
4 eggs	1/2 pound chopped almonds

Mix yeast and milk, and stir in 1 cup flour. Let rise. Cream butter with sugar. Add eggs one at a time, beat well, and add lemon rind, and salt. Combine two mixtures. Add nutmeg and remaining flour and knead until smooth and elastic. Sprinkle rum over dried fruits. Mix and add to dough with nuts. Let rise until doubled. On floured board, divide dough into three or more loaves. Roll out each loaf slightly, spread top with melted butter, press down the center, and fold over double. Brush again

with melted butter and let rise until doubled. Bake at 350°
F, about 45 minutes. When slightly cool, cover with
plain icing.
NOTE: The folds, which are meant to represent the folds
in the Christ child's swaddling clothes, should remain
visible.

Slovak Christmas treats:

PIROHY

1 cup flour
1 egg
1/4 teaspoon salt
about 4 tablespoons cold water
butter, melted and slightly browned

Mix flour, egg, and salt with enough water to make a
medium soft dough. Knead well, then roll out thin. Cut
in squares to make about 4 dozen *pirohy*. Place 1 teaspoon filling of your choice (listed below) on each
square. Moisten edges of *pirohy* slightly with water. Fold
in half to make triangles. Pinch edges well to keep filling
from escaping. Drop in salted, gently boiling water and
cook until all *pirohy* rise to the surface. Cook for 5 minutes longer. Remove to colander and rinse with small
amount of cold water. Place *pirohy* in serving dish and
top with butter that has been melted and slightly
browned.

PIROHY FILLINGS

Cheese: Combine 1/2 cup dry cottage cheese, 1 egg yolk,
1 teaspoon butter, and a pinch of salt.

Potato: Peel, cook, and mash one large potato. Add one tablespoon melted butter, and salt to taste. Other flavorings such as basil, rosemary, cheddar cheese may be added.

Prune: Cook and mash prunes, or use *lekvar*, a commercial, ready-made prune mixture.

Cabbage: Chop a one-pound head of cabbage fine. Salt and set aside for several minutes. Squeeze out water and saute cabbage in small amount of butter or margarine until soft and golden brown.

KOLACHE (GRANDMA YUHAS' RECIPE)

3 packages dry yeast	5 eggs, beaten
3/4 cup warm milk	1-1/2 cups sour cream
3/4 pound margarine	9 cups flour
6 tablespoons sugar	1-1/2 teaspoons salt

Dissolve yeast in milk. Combine margarine, sugar, eggs and sour cream. Stir in flour and salt. Add yeast and milk mixture. Blend well. Divide dough into three parts and roll out each part fairly thin (approximately 12 x 18 inches). Spread with nut, poppyseed, and/or pineapple-raisin filling. Roll up (jelly roll-style), place on greased pan, and allow to rise for one hour or until double. Bake 35 to 40 minutes at 350° F.

KOLACHE FILLINGS

Each of the following makes enough to fill about four rolls.

Nut Filling. Heat in a saucepan until just warm:

1 to 1-1/2 pounds ground walnuts
3/4 cup raisins (optional)

1 tablespoon lemon juice
1/2 cup brown sugar or honey, or to taste
milk (enough to make mixture easy to spread)

Poppyseed Filling. Heat in a saucepan until just warm:

1 pound ground poppyseed
1 cup raisins, chopped
1/2 cup honey, or to taste
1 teaspoon vanilla (optional)
milk (enough to make mixture easy to spread)

Pineapple-Raisin Filling (a favorite of our family).

1 cup raisins
1 20 oz. can crushed pineapple, including syrup
1/2 cup sugar, or to taste
2 tablespoons cornstarch
1/2 cup cold water

Heat raisins, pineapple, and sugar stirring constantly in a saucepan until they come to a slow, rolling boil. Mix corn starch with water in a small bowl until cornstarch disolves. When raisin mixture boils, add the disolved corn starch. Stir until thickened.

CHAPTER 4

~

THE LENTEN SEASON
Ash Wednesday through
Holy Saturday

The Lenten season is an intense period of penitential practices, designed to awaken in us a greater sense of our need for the redemption brought by Christ's crucifixion on Good Friday.

Lent represents the forty days in the wilderness that Jesus took to prepare himself for his public ministry and his death and resurrection. It also recalls the forty years when the ancient Israelites wandered in the desert after their deliverance from Egypt and before their entrance into the promised land—years of testing and purification.

Ash Wednesday, the first day of Lent, is a good time to examine our consciences and to select our Lenten sacrifices and activities. With God's grace, these will bring us closer to Jesus and make us better instruments of his plans for the kingdom.

It is easy to think of Lent as a dismal time of penance and fasting. To make the most of this season, however, take some time before it begins to ponder its deeper meaning and mystery.

Lent encourages us to draw closer to Christ through sorrow for sin and repentance. What might this mean in your life? Do you want to be closer to Christ? More loving to those around you? Could Lent help you to battle pride and sinfulness and come to a gradual acceptance of God's special plan for you? How can you best prepare your soul to understand God's personal message to you?

∼ *Traditions for the Season of Lent* ∼

Almsgiving. Like Advent, Lent is a time for almsgiving and other kinds of sharing. During Advent our giving is especially inspired by gratitude for the great gift of Jesus himself to the human race. During Lent we give sacrificially, remembering how Christ gave his life for us.

Operation Rice Bowl is the name of one Lenten program that some Catholic families and parishes adopt during Lent. (St. Joseph's Table is another.) Participants in Operation Rice Bowl choose one day each week of Lent—often a Wednesday or Friday—on which they substitute a meal of soup and bread or some other simple fare for their usual dinner. They then estimate the difference in cost between this simple dinner and their usual repast and donate that money to the poor—in this case, through Catholic Relief Services, the charitable organization that sponsors this program.

You may want to try introducing your family to Operation Rice Bowl for Lent. If so, you can use this prayer from Catholic Relief Services:

Throughout Lent, we prepare for the celebration of the resurrection of Jesus. Our Lenten fasting reminds us of our sisters and brothers who are without food or drink. Let us be ready to share with them from our table. May God bless this Lenten gift from our family to our sisters and brothers. May we continue to remember them as we strive to give hope to a world in need. Amen.

Upon request, Catholic Relief Services will provide a special container in which to collect your Lenten alms. (Twenty-five percent of whatever money you donate to CRS will be used to help the poor in your diocese.)[1]

Other good almsgiving practices for Lent: donate clothes, games, food, and other useful items to the needy; prepare a meal for the homeless; help stock a local foodshelf for the poor.

Confession. The Church requires only those Catholics who are in a state of serious sin to make a good confession during the Lenten or Easter season. But for most Catholics, going to confession is a customary part of preparing for Easter. Many parishes facilitate this by organizing Lenten penance services: priests from other parishes are brought in for a penance service followed by individual confessions.

Lenten fasts. Fasting during Lent recalls Jesus' fast for forty days in the wilderness. For Catholics ages eighteen to sixty, Ash Wednesday and Good Friday are designated days of fasting, which means eating only one full meal and two lighter meals. On the same days and on all the Fridays of Lent, Catholics fourteen and over are also obliged to abstain from meat. (A modified fast is recommended for people who are elderly, ill, or in situations where fasting would be difficult. Medicines and other necessities are not prohibited.)

In the Eastern rites of the Catholic Church, Lenten fasting is much more common than in the Western rites. God's will regarding the degree of fast for each person is discerned in prayer. (At what age a child begins to fast during Lent is decided individually with the pastor, who usually knows all the families in his parish.) Some fasts allow only bread, water, nuts, and fruit; others eliminate only meat, or only dairy products and meat; in others, everything is eaten except dairy products, meat, fish, wine and oil.

Lenten prayers. Lent is an especially good time for extra prayer. You might try to get up early to pray and read Scripture. During that time you could also think about ways to improve your behavior during the day: how to snap at others less, how to befriend the lonely, how to grow in patience.

Lenten programs. Catholic bookstores often sell booklets with well-worked-out Lenten programs for the family. You might look through such materials for ideas to use in your home.

Lenten resolutions. It is customary to make resolutions involving various kinds of penance or acts of charity during the season of Lent. (Our family's custom was to suggest resolutions for one another.) Some Catholics might give up something like candy. Others try to fast from a habit such as gossiping. Another possibility is to volunteer to help with chores or some other task.

Or you might clean out closets and drawers, giving away serviceable items to the poor. In some families these penitential practices are suspended on Sundays during Lent.

To help motivate younger children with their resolutions, some parents have each child make a "Lenten Mouse" out of felt with a long, string tail. Each time the child makes a Lenten sacrifice or does a good deed, mom or dad ties a knot in the mouse's tail.

Pilgrimages. In Rome the custom arose of visiting designated pilgrimage churches during Lent. You can adapt this custom by visiting whatever places of pilgrimage may be in your area. You can also visit other Catholic churches, especially those that continue the religious traditions of Catholics from other nationalities. Check with the offices of your diocese or archdiocese for a listing of churches near you.

Stations of the cross. You can buy or make stations of the cross. (See chapter seven for a fuller explanation of this devotion.) Run the stations up the staircase or simply place them around a room. Make up your own prayers for each station, or use those provided in special booklets (available at Catholic bookstores). Pray the stations every Friday, either as a group or by taking turns. It is a Hispanic custom to perform the stations on one's knees during Lent.

Statue covers. Before Vatican II, churches would cover statues with purple cloth during Lent (purple is the color that symbolizes penance). You can adopt this tradition by covering the religious statues and pictures in your home, as a reminder to persevere in Lenten prayer and sacrifice.

∼ *Special Days of the Season* ∼

Ash Wednesday. Ash Wednesday, the beginning of Lent, recalls the Old Testament practice of doing penance in sackcloth and ashes. Chapter three of the Book of Jonah gives a graphic account of how the people of Nineveh did penance wearing sackcloth and covering themselves with ashes as a sign of repentance for their sins.

On Ash Wednesday we receive ashes as a sign of penitence. They are made from the burning of the palm branches which have been saved from the previous Palm Sunday. (On this day, it is especially appropriate to burn any palm branches you have around the house or to return them to church to be burned.) Since these ashes are sacramentals, some groups of Catholics—Hispanics, for example—put a great emphasis on going to church on Ash Wednesday to receive them.

In the Greek Catholic Church, holy oil is blessed on Ash Wednesday. The people take some home and use it to anoint themselves and others during the year.

Palm Sunday (Passion Sunday). The celebration of Palm Sunday began in the fourth century in Jerusalem, at the very place where the crowd acclaimed Jesus as king. As this celebration evolved, the bishop would ride a donkey up to the church on the Mount of Olives, with the crowd carrying palms and singing hymns.

You can usually obtain at the Palm Sunday service in your church blessed palm or olive branches to use in your prayer nook or devotional area. Bring in the family crucifix and take turns draping the branches over it. Some families braid the palms and put them around the crucifix.

On Palm Sunday in the Philippines, each corner of the church features designs of palms of different types. Mass is preceded by a long outdoor procession of people carrying palms and singing hymns.

The Triduum (Holy Thursday, Good Friday, and Holy Saturday). These are the holiest days of the year and should be viewed as one continuous liturgy. Many families go to church together each day of the Triduum. (If you have some children who are too young to attend, you and your spouse can take turns coming with the older children.)

In addition to the special liturgies of the day, some churches have reinstituted morning prayers during the Triduum. If you do not have the opportunity to attend these, you and other family members can pray at home, perhaps using the Liturgy of the Hours. (More on these prayers in chapter seven.)

In Austria during the Triduum, altar boys race through the streets with a special rattle called a *Ratschen* to remind the people to pray.

Holy Thursday. Also known as Maundy Thursday, this day commemorates the Last Supper, when Jesus first gave his disciples the Eucharist. It is a tradition for devout Catholics to go to the Holy Thursday services. Afterwards some adults like to pray into the night at the special Blessed Sacrament altar, where the consecrated hosts are kept for the next day's service. In some churches, members of the congregation may dress in biblical costumes and sit around a table enacting the Last Supper.

A rather new custom that is becoming more and more common is to hold some kind of Passover service before the Mass, either at home or in the parish hall.[2] This is based on the Jewish Passover meal that Christ shared with his apostles at the Last Supper. It is usually accompanied by some commentary explaining the meaning of the rituals and their significance for Christians. The Jewish Passover service can be obtained from any Jewish bookstore. Christian commentary services can be obtained from the Hebrew-Catholic Association.[3]

In the Philippines on Holy Thursday, members of the congregation dress up as Jesus' disciples and stand around the life-size statues of Jesus and Mary in the church.

In Mexico, it is customary to visit the "Seven Houses." These are churches, monuments, or convents which are open to worshipers after the Holy Thursday services. Each one displays a beautiful "altar of repose" as a sort of throne for a huge, consecrated host. (In fact, there is a kind of rivalry as to which churches will make the most beautiful altars.) Children are sometimes very curious about what convents are really like inside, and this adds to their enjoyment of these Holy Thursday visits!

Good Friday. Good Friday is when we remember Jesus' death on the cross for our sins. Like Holy Thursday,

Good Friday is not a day of obligation, but many Catholics attend the day's services. Many also participate in praying the stations of the cross at church. (This devotion is described in chapter seven.)

Good Friday is a day when it is traditional for Catholics to pray for the souls in purgatory. Appropriate prayers for the dead, some with special indulgences, can be obtained from Catholic bookstores. (See chapter seven for an explanation of indulgences.)

To maintain a spirit of prayer and reflection, some families keep the radio and television off on Good Friday. Others take on a special activity such as preparing a meal for the homeless.

In Mexico during this time, churches feature statues of Christ that focus on his suffering and death. One shows him crowned with thorns; another shows him carrying the cross; in another, a replica of the dead Christ is displayed in a large coffin. On Good Friday, this last statue is laid in a grave filled with flowers. All through the night and into the next day, people come to visit Christ at this shrine and to pray.

A similar custom of making a grave for Christ is also observed in Austria. In the Philippines, a figure of Christ is buried in a freshly-made papier-mâché tomb.

In southern Spain, there are elaborate Good Friday processions. People lean off balconies and cry out dirges and petition prayers (*saetas*).

Holy Saturday. Easter begins on the evening of Holy Saturday with the Easter Vigil Mass. This is one of the most moving and dramatic ceremonies of the church year. It is at this Mass that new converts are received into the Church after months of preparation and special classes (through the Rite of Christian Initiation for Adults, or "RCIA"). At the Easter Vigil, those new members who have never received the sacrament (catechumens) are baptized, those already baptized (candidates) are confirmed, and all receive the Eucharist for the first time.

Because the Easter Vigil services usually go on for two or three hours, many parents choose not to bring small children. One way in which families can participate in the event, however, is by "sponsoring" a catechumen or a candidate—giving special help in understanding and living out the Catholic faith. Those who are unable to do this may enjoy simply befriending one of these new members of the Church, perhaps inviting him or her to brunch at home after Mass. Family devotions is a good time to pray for those people who are learning about the Catholic faith.

∼ *Other Special Days during Lent* ∼

Chair of St. Peter, Apostle ....February 22
St. Patrick ....March 17
St. Joseph ....March 19

∼ *For Your Family* ∼

There is lots of opportunity for family interaction during the Lenten season. You might try family Passion plays on Good Friday, dramatic reenactments of the stations of the cross every Friday, or praying the sorrowful mysteries of the rosary together every week.

Family Day. This is a good way to prepare for Lent. Choose a day to spend together before the season begins. After breakfast, work together as a family to make posters listing traits of Jesus: patience, kindness, and so on. Talk about which of these qualities you need more of in your own lives.

During the day, everyone should look for ways to help another person in the family (volunteer to do someone's least favorite chore, perhaps, or watch younger children so mom can have some free time).

After lunch you can have a discussion in which each person mentions some of the qualities they appreciate in the other members of the family. End with a group prayer thanking God for one another.

In the evening after dinner, gather together and have each family member ask the others for suggestions about Lenten resolutions.

Plan special family devotions for Holy Week. Do something as a family each day of the Triduum to remember the Passion of Christ.

On Maundy Thursday you might prepare a Passover meal. Or bring Easter lilies to the special Eucharistic altar in your church.

On Good Friday, watch a video of the life of Jesus with your family (Franco Zeffirelli's *Jesus of Nazareth* is a good choice). Put a small statue or picture of Michelangelo's *Piéta* in your devotional area, or set up a cross with a stand. Good Friday is also an opportunity to give family members small crosses they can wear on a chain or carry in a pocket or purse.

On Holy Saturday, family members who cannot attend the Easter Vigil might try putting together a dramatic reenactment of the Resurrection.

A family Passion play, presented during Holy Week and the Easter season, is an effective way to help even small children prepare for and celebrate the feast. Some families focus on the story of Jesus' death, while others retell the whole story, from the Garden of Gethsemane through the Resurrection.

Bake hot cross buns. In England, people make these spiced buns for Good Friday or Ash Wednesday. (Some people eat them for breakfast on Easter Sunday.)

HOT CROSS BUNS

1 cup scalded milk
1/4 cup sugar
1 egg
1 tablespoon lemon juice
1/4 cup butter or margarine
1 package dry yeast
3 1/2 cups flour
2 teaspoons salt
1 1/2 tsp grated lemon rind
1/2 cup raisins
1 egg, (well beaten, for top of buns)

In a large bowl, stir milk, sugar, egg, lemon juice, and butter until blended. Add yeast and stir. Add 2-1/2 cups flour, salt, and lemon rind and beat well. Cover, put in a warm place and leave for an hour. Add raisins and knead, adding enough of the remaining flour to make a smooth dough. Cover loosely in warm, greased bowl until doubled in size. Punch down. Form dough into buns and place on greased pan, at least 1 inch apart. Cut a cross on the tops and brush with beaten egg. Let rise until double in size. Bake in preheated 375° F oven for 20 minutes. When buns are cool, pipe icing onto the crosses.

ICING

3 egg whites
1 tablespoon lemon juice
1-1/2 cups powdered sugar

To make icing, beat egg whites and lemon juice in a bowl. Gradually add powdered sugar until icing is stiff.

CHAPTER 5

THE EASTER SEASON
Easter Sunday through Pentecost

Easter is the season of great rejoicing in the Church, the glorious time when we celebrate the resurrection of Christ. It begins with the Easter Vigil and continues for fifty days, through Pentecost. The Easter season marks the high point of the liturgical year, because during this time we celebrate both Jesus' resurrection and, through it, our restored relationship with God. As one of the Eucharistic acclamations used at Mass puts it: "Dying, you destroyed our death. Rising, you restored our life."

∼ *Traditions for the Easter Season* ∼

Chanting the psalms. Before Vatican II, devout Catholics would spend the mornings of Holy Thursday, Good Friday, and Holy Saturday in church, where the psalms were chanted. Now some parishes have introduced an abbreviated form of this custom by holding morning prayer in the church. Individuals or groups who cannot attend these services can still pray the psalms for the day by obtaining a copy of *The Liturgy of the Hours*. (This prayer of the Church is explained in chapter seven.)

Easter dinner. It is most customary to eat lamb on Easter Sunday, celebrating the resurrection of the Lamb of God. It is a Slovakian custom to eat ham and sausages called *kielbasi*. In Italy, marzipan candies are a traditional Easter treat.

Easter eggs. From the tenth century, the foods one fasted from during Lent—eggs, for example—made a glorious reappearance at Easter. Eggs are certainly prominent in our celebrations of the feast today: we hunt them, decorate them, and eat them in many forms. Catholics like to decorate Easter eggs with religious symbols, such as a triangle for the Trinity, or with a picture of Jesus coming out of the tomb. The egg symbolizes the Resurrection: when a chick is enclosed in the shell, as in a tomb, it must break out into life; so too, Jesus broke out of his tomb. The fertilized egg looks dead but is full of life.

Easter fire. In Austria, people light bonfires on the mountains in honor of the risen Lord.

Easter lilies. These beautiful flowers, which come from dead-looking bulbs buried in the ground, symbolize resurrection. Many Catholics decorate their homes with Easter lilies and other flowers to celebrate the joy of Easter.

Easter parade. An old European custom is to parade in a procession after Mass. A cross and an Easter candle are carried at the head of the procession.

Easter plays. Some families read the story of Easter together after Easter dinner; others have family members act it out. In our family, we liked to tell the story with puppets. (See "Carla's Easter Play" in the "For Your Home" section of this chapter.)

In the Philippines, it is traditional for parishes to present an Easter play. Actors playing Christ and the disciples come to the tomb, which is painted on a backdrop in the church.

Glorious mysteries. It is traditional to pray the glorious mysteries of the rosary during the Easter season.

∼ Traditions for the Special Days ∼ following Easter

Mercy Sunday. This somewhat recently authorized feast day is celebrated on the first Sunday after Easter. This devotion derives from an apparition to Sr. Faustina, a Polish nun who was recently beatified. In her convent in Poland in 1931, she saw a vision of Jesus with rays of light coming from his garments. Jesus asked her to have a picture made of this vision, with these words on it: "Jesus, I trust in thee." Called the Divine Mercy, this image is now venerated in many countries.

Sr. Faustina also received from Jesus the prayers for what is called the Divine Mercy chaplet. Reciting the chaplet has become more and more popular among Catholics, especially on Mercy Sunday. (See chapter seven, "Mercy Prayers," for information on how to pray this chaplet.)

The Ascension. The Ascension, which is celebrated forty days after Easter, commemorates the day the disciples saw Jesus taken up into heaven. It is the custom of some families to go to the nearest mountain on this day and enact the scene (in which people may groan or praise God as they "see" Jesus rising) or read the following Scripture:

> When he had said this, as they were watching, he was lifted up, and a cloud took him out of their sight. While he was going and they were gazing up toward heaven, suddenly two men in white robes stood by them. They said, "Men of Galilee, why do you stand looking up toward heaven? This Jesus, who has been taken up from you into heaven, will come in the same way as you saw him go into heaven." ACTS 1:9-11

The Swiss have a charming custom for celebrating Ascension Thursday. Before the day's liturgy a statue of the risen Lord is suspended on a wire over the altar. After the reading of the Gospel at Mass, this statue is pulled by its wire through a hole that can be seen above the altar in many old churches in the Alps.

There are Swiss traditions for Pentecost too. On the Saturday before the feast young men go out and crack long whips or shoot off old cannons. These loud noises are supposed to signify the sounds of the coming of the Holy Spirit. Some Catholics walk barefoot into the mountains through the dew on Pentecost morning, calling for the Holy Spirit to come. A dove is let into the church through the hole above the altar during Pentecost Mass, symbolizing the coming of the Holy Spirit into the midst of the Christians gathered together on the first Pentecost.

Pentecost is celebrated fifty days after Easter and is the last day of the Church's Easter season. This is the time when Catholics celebrate the coming of the Holy Spirit to Mary, the apostles, and the disciples (Acts 2:1-4). We share in the gifts of the Holy Spirit, reflect on what they have meant and now mean for the Church, and pray for those gifts of the Spirit that we don't have. These gifts include the permanent gifts of the Spirit and the charismatic gifts of the Spirit.

Permanent gifts of the Spirit. These gifts are mentioned in chapter eleven of the Book of Isaiah to describe the Messiah. With the coming of Christ and the sending of the Holy Spirit, followers of Jesus receive a share in these gifts. They include:

- wisdom (to value the things of heaven over those of earth)
- understanding (to comprehend religious truth)
- counsel (to choose well in serving God)
- fortitude (to make sacrifices in living the faith)
- knowledge (to follow the way of the Lord)
- piety (to put one's trust in God)
- fear of the Lord (to give God and his laws due respect)

In some families, there is a sharing time after dinner on Pentecost and during the week following. Each member discusses how to use these spiritual gifts in daily life. For example, every time you choose to pray for even a few moments instead of rushing out to do your own thing, the Holy Spirit is helping you to use the gift of wisdom. Each gift can be illustrated by many such practical examples.

Charismatic gifts of the Spirit. The charismatic gifts mentioned in 1 Corinthians 12 are granted primarily as helps for the upbuilding of the Church and include:

- prophecy (speaking in the name of the Lord)
- tongues (praying in a language that is unknown to the speaker)
- interpretation of tongues
- healing
- word of knowledge (uttering a truth needed by another which could not be known by any usual means).

In some cities, charismatic prayer groups arrange a special Pentecost Mass. Or in the weeks preceding Pentecost, they may organize Life in the Spirit Seminars to open people to the charismatic gifts of the Spirit, received in potency at confirmation but not always brought to the surface.

Some families focus in prayer during Pentecost on remaining open to the charismatic gifts of the Spirit.

Pentecost Novena. This beautiful novena prayer can be said for the nine days prior to Pentecost.

Come O Holy Spirit, fill the hearts of your faithful and
    kindle in them the fire of your love.
Send forth your Spirit
And they shall be created
And you will renew the face of the earth.
O God, our Father, you teach your family through the
    light of your Holy Spirit. Grant that by the same Spirit
    we may be truly wise, and always rejoice in his
    consolation, through Christ, our Lord. Amen.

There are two very ancient Latin hymns to the Holy
Spirit. The following versions are free translations in
prose form.

O Creator Spirit of God, come to those
    who belong to you and fill them with your grace.
You are called "the helper," "the Father's gift," "the living
    spring," a "fire," "a spiritual comfort."
You give us your aid in seven different ways, for you are
    the power of God, promised by him, to help us speak
    and pray.
Enlighten our minds, warm our hearts, and with your
    power strengthen our weakness.
Keep our enemy away from us. Give us peace, so that
    with you as our guide, we may be delivered from all
    that is evil.
We pray that through you we may know the Father and
    Son.
We believe that you are the Spirit of love uniting them.
Glory be to the Father, and to the Son, who rose from the
    dead, and to you, our helper, for ever and ever. Amen.

*Come, O Holy Spirit, and shine on us the rays of your
     light.*
*You are a father to the poor. Come, then, giver of
     presents, come to us, you who are the light
     of men's minds.*
*You are the best of all friends, a man's gracious guest
     and companion.*
*You offer rest to those who labor, shelter to
     those who look for shade,
     comfort to those who are sad.*
O blessed light, fill the hearts of all Christians.
*Without you a man is an empty shell,
     unable to do any good.*
*Wash away whatever is unclean in man,
     refresh whatever is parched,
     heal whatever is wounded,
     soften whatever is unyielding,
     warm whatever is cold,
     rule whatever is unruly.*
Give your seven gifts to all those who rely on you.
*Give them the reward of good living,
     salvation and joy for ever. Amen.*[1]

∼ Other Special Days during the Season ∼

∼ *For Your Home* ∼

Listen to Easter dinner music! Play Gregorian chants or great classical music pieces such as Handel's *Messiah* on Easter Sunday.

Put on an Easter play. Perhaps you or another family member would enjoy writing a simple play that tells the Easter story. Or you can use this puppet presentation, a custom in our family: "Carla's Easter Play." Puppets can be created by attaching magazine pictures or hand-drawn figures to Popsicle sticks. Backgrounds can be made from poster board or any other materials you have around the house.

[Curtain opens to reveal Saint Peter puppet alone, fishing.]

PETER: Oh! Hello! I'm just here fishing, thinking about old times. My name is Peter by the way, Simon Peter. Once I was just Simon the fisherman. Then HE came along. But of course, you know that story, right?

[If there is no response, he should ask again, perhaps calling an audience member by name.]

Well, it's a good story. If you want, I'll tell you again while I fish. Okay? Fine. Let me see now... where to begin?

Once upon a time, there was this man called Jesus... he was the Son of God—although most people knew him as the son of Mary and Joseph, the carpenter from Nazareth. As a man, Jesus went around telling everyone he saw about God, his Father, and performing miracles—like healing sick people! A couple of times, he even made dead people come to life again!

I was glad that happened—and so were many, many people. But there were some religious leaders, called Pharisees...

[up Pharisee puppet]

who didn't believe that Jesus was God's son, and the things that he said and did made them very angry! They were so angry, they made plans to kill Jesus.

[Pharisee puppet disappears.]

Jesus knew all about this and worried about us. So one day, he decided to talk to his best friends over dinner.

[Close curtain, put up Last Supper background. Jesus puppet and Peter puppet on stage.]

There's Jesus, right here *[nods at Jesus]*. Anyway, I was at that dinner. Jesus said a lot of interesting things. Why don't you listen with me for a minute.

JESUS: Verily, I say unto you that one of you shall betray me.

PETER: Yeah, well that's the way we talked in those days. He's saying that one of his friends was really a bad man in disguise. Of course, he meant the one we called Judas, but we didn't know that then. Next, he told us he was inside the bread and wine. Let's listen some more.

JESUS: Take, eat; this is my body. *[pause]* Drink ye all of it. For this is the blood of the new testament, which is shed for many for the remission of sins.

PETER: And that was the first Communion. When you're old enough, you'll go to Communion at Mass.

[Close curtain, take down Last Supper background, put up Garden. Peter and Jesus are on stage, Jesus is by himself in the Garden.]

PETER: After dinner, Jesus went into a garden called Gethsemane with his friends. He knew that the bad men would kill him if they found him, but Jesus wanted to obey what his Father said he must do.

JESUS: Oh my Father, if this cup may not pass away from me, except I drink it, thy will be done.

PETER: Meanwhile, Judas had been talking with the bad men. They wanted to know which one was Jesus so they could take him away. Judas said he would kiss the one who was Jesus.

[Bring up Judas puppet. Judas kisses Jesus, then disappears. Soldier puppet comes up, then both soldier and Jesus disappear.]

The bad men took Jesus to the head of the bad men called Pontius Pilate.

[Pilate appears on stage.]

PILATE: What shall I do with Jesus who is called Christ?

Many different voices, one after another: Crucify him!

[Pilate disappears.]

PETER: That means put him on a cross until he dies.

[Close curtain, put up cross backdrop. Soldier and Jesus puppet are on stage, Jesus in front of the cross on backdrop, as though he is nailed to it already.]

So the bad men came and nailed Jesus to a cross. Some of his friends waited, hoping that Jesus would do one more miracle and save himself.

[Close curtain. Peter stands in front.]

But nothing happened. When Jesus died, they took him down from the cross and gave him to his mama.

[Open curtain. Cave backdrop, with Mary in front of the cave.]

That's her there. She's called Mary. Then they put his body in a cave. We were all very sad. I remember that I cried and cried because Jesus was gone.

[Close curtain. Peter in front.]

The next day, some women came to see his body. He was not in the cave! We thought that all the bad men must have stolen him!

[Open curtain. Stone at the mouth of tomb is rolled away from the door. Jesus puppet in front.]

But later we found out this wasn't true. Jesus was alive! We saw him! We knew then that he was God's Son for sure, and that he was going to save the world!

JESUS: Lo! I am with you always, even unto the end of the world. Amen.

[Jesus puppet disappears. Peter puppet appears.]

PETER: And that's the end of the story. Or really... the beginning!

[Close curtain.]

Have special prayers at Pentecost. Read 1 Corinthians 12:4-11 together. Talk about the gifts of the Spirit and tell stories about how you have seen them in action. Pray over each person for openness to the Holy Spirit. Here is a traditional prayer of the Church that you may want to include at your meeting:

Come, Holy Spirit, fill the hearts of your faithful,
and kindle in them the fire of your love.
Send forth your Spirit, and they shall be created
and you will renew the face of the earth! [2]

Start a Eucharistic home shrine. Corpus Christi is a good day to encourage a family tradition of adoring Jesus in the Eucharist. One way to do this is through the Eucharistic Home Shrine movement,[3] now known on seven continents. A family or community sets up a Eucharistic home shrine by putting up a special picture, designed by the founder of the movement to inspire thanksgiving and reparation to the Eucharistic Heart of Jesus and the Sorrowful and Immaculate Heart of Mary.

This picture reminds everyone that the Lord loves them and wishes them to respond to him by frequent reception of Holy Communion. At each Mass, members of the Eucharistic Home Shrine movement pray that Christ would visit all the home shrines in a special way and bless everyone in each family or group.

CHAPTER 6

ORDINARY TIME AND FEAST DAYS

Family Days throughout the Year

Whatever does not fall into the seasons of Advent, Christmas, Lent, and Easter in the church calendar comes under the heading of Ordinary Time. Within this period there are many feast days. Some commemorate special times in the life of the holy family; others mark the births or deaths or peak moments in the lives of the saints (such as the conversion of St. Paul).

Catholics who attend daily Mass are familiar with such feast days, as are those who pray the Liturgy of the Hours each day. Eastern rite Catholics celebrate major feast days not only on the day of the feast but also throughout the week by chanting the prayers of that day for six days afterward.

This chapter includes Catholic customs and traditions that regularly take place in connection with the feast days we think are most universally popular. It also includes religious practices for holidays that are not inherently Catholic but that have spiritual significance.

We have included activities and prayers that are appropriate for each holiday or feast day. You can also create your own family or community traditions—for example, feast day celebrations for saints you especially love who have not been included in our book.

~ *Special Days during Ordinary Time* ~

Feast of the Body and Blood of Christ (Corpus Christi). This feast is celebrated in the United States on the second Sunday after Pentecost and commemorates the institution of the Holy Eucharist. In the past, Catholics would be sure to go to Mass individually or as a family to celebrate how Jesus instituted the sacrament of Holy Communion in order to come right into our bodies with his sacred body and blood. As has often been said, since God made the whole universe out of nothing, he can certainly arrange for his Son's body and blood to invade, as it were, a little piece of bread.

The evening before or after, you might gather to share about your experiences of finding strength from Holy Communion. As a group, you might also pray the Liturgy of the Hours for the feast of Corpus Christi; it was composed by St. Thomas Aquinas.

In many countries it is the custom to have a Corpus Christi procession. The priest, dressed in ceremonial robes, carries the Blessed Sacrament through the streets, accompanied by altar boys and girls dressed up in communion dresses. A band plays and sometimes flowers are strewn in the streets and bells are rung. In the United States, which is not a Catholic country, such processions are sometimes confined to the church grounds.

Sacred Heart of Jesus (Friday following Second Sunday after Pentecost). Over the centuries, as Christ has taught his Church through the ministry of his saints, there have been many revelations concerning the love burning in the heart of Jesus for his beloved children. The feast of the Sacred Heart celebrates the most famous of these. In his appearances to St. Margaret Mary Alacoque, a French nun of the seventeenth century, Jesus made the following twelve promises to those who would respond to the love in his heart with devotion:

1. I will give them all the graces necessary for their state of life.

2. I will give peace in their families.

3. I will console them in all their troubles.

4. They shall find in my heart an assured refuge during life and especially at the hour of death.

5. I will pour abundant blessings on all their undertakings.

6. Sinners shall find in my heart the source and infinite ocean of mercy.

7. Tepid souls shall become fervent.

8. Fervent souls shall speedily rise to great perfection.

9. I will bless the homes in which the image of my Sacred Heart shall be exposed and honored.

10. I will give to priests the power to touch the most hardened hearts.

11. Those who propagate this devotion shall have their name written in my heart, and it shall never be effaced.

12. The all-powerful love of my heart will grant to all those who shall receive communion on the first Friday of nine consecutive months the grace of final repentance; they shall not die under my displeasure, nor without receiving their sacraments; my heart shall be their assured refuge at that last hour.

Catholics with a devotion to the Sacred Heart of Jesus customarily recite the litany to the Sacred Heart on this day. It is becoming a popular custom for families to consecrate themselves as a group to the Sacred Heart in a ceremony known as enthronement of the Sacred Heart. (See this entry in chapter seven.)

Immaculate Heart of Mary (Saturday following Second Sunday after Pentecost). On this day many Catholics observe the custom of making or renewing a consecration of themselves to the Immaculate Heart of Mary. Various saints and contemplatives have said that Mary makes special promises to those who make the consecration and follow through by frequent Holy Communion and confession: their names will be written in the hearts of Jesus and Mary, and they and their family members will be saved because they will receive special graces to repent of sin.

Here is one act of consecration, written by St. Louis Marie de Montfort:[1]

I, (name), a faithless sinner, renew and ratify today in thy hands the vows of my Baptism; I renounce forever Satan, his pomps and works; and I give myself entirely to Jesus Christ, the Incarnate Wisdom, to carry my cross after Him all the days of my life, and to be more faithful to Him than I have ever been before.

In the presence of all the heavenly court I choose thee this day for my Mother and Mistress. I deliver and consecrate to thee, as thy slave, my body and soul, my goods, both interior and exterior, and even the value of all my good actions, past, present, and future; leaving to thee the entire and full right of disposing of me, and all that belongs to me, without exception, according to thy good pleasure, for the greater glory of God, in time and in eternity. Amen.

A shorter form of consecration, especially useful for small children, is this: *"O Mary, my queen and my mother, remember I am all yours. Keep me and guard me as your property and possession. Amen."*

Feast of the Holy Family (Sunday within the octave of Christmas or, if there is none, December 29). This beautiful feast celebrates the virtues of Mary and Joseph, their trust in God's protection, and their loving interaction as together they cared for the child Jesus. During the family devotional time on this day everyone might discuss which member of the holy family they can most identify with. Conclude the devotional time with the following prayer:

Jesus, Mary, Joseph, we love you. Save us and bring us to the heavenly kingdom where all will be joy and happiness and love.

∽ Holidays and Feast Days Throughout ∽ the Year (by month)

JANUARY

Solemnity of Mary, Mother of God (January 1, day of obligation). This feast day celebrates the maternity of Mary. To honor her, you could display a statue of Mary or a picture of Mary with the infant Jesus and place a candle before it. Some families have a tradition of collecting different images of Our Lady—folk art, icons, reproductions of classical paintings. On this day you might begin a scrapbook of such pictures or a display of Marian art on one wall in your house. On this day and other major feasts, many devout families make it a rule to keep the TV off.

In Germany, the family usually begins the day by going together to Mass. Later at home there are special petitions for the New Year, treats of marzipan mushrooms, and good luck tokens for the children, followed by a special lunch.

Feast of the Holy Name of Jesus (January 4). The name of Jesus is for Christians the most beautiful word in the world. Just repeating the name of Jesus is a powerful prayer. In fact, the simplest form of the Jesus Prayer (or Prayer of the Heart), which is a special tradition of the Orthodox, consists of simply repeating the name of Jesus over and over throughout the day.

Many Catholics have adopted this practice, sometimes praying the Jesus Prayer intensely during a specific prayer time and then letting it flow from the heart to the mind in the midst of daily activities. (See chapter seven, "Offering Up.") This feast day might be a time to learn about this prayer or teach it to others.

Another prayer you can use—perhaps during your grace at dinner—is this invocation to the Holy Name:

"O admirable Name of Jesus! Name most holy! To us most amiable! Name above every name. No other name is given under heaven in which we can be saved.

"Jesus, honey in our mouth, melody in our ears, sweet jubilee to our hearts! O Jesus! you are our life, you are our salvation, you are our glory; to you be praise forever and ever. Amen."

Martin Luther King Day (January 17). This can be a good day for the family to go to Mass or to organize a prayer service at home around the message of Martin Luther King. You might pray for minority groups of all kinds, especially those in your own region. You could also watch a video tape or TV program about Dr. King, and talk about Christianity and non-violence in society and at home.

Conversion of St. Paul (January 25). The story of how Saul the persecutor of Christians became Paul the follower of Christ is one of the most dramatic of the New Testament. At dinnertime on January 25th, one of the members of your family could read the account in Acts 9:1-9. Then you might all share about times when you have felt very surprised by the Holy Spirit. Young people might enjoy making up a skit about this great event.

FEBRUARY

Presentation of the Lord (February 2). When Mary and Joseph brought Jesus to Jerusalem to present him in the temple, the prophet Simeon told them that Jesus would be "a light for revelation to the Gentiles" (Lk 2:32). This is why blessed candles are distributed to churchgoers on this feast. Keep these blessed candles in your prayer area. You can light them on special days, such as anniversaries of baptisms of family members or the feasts of the saints after whom they are named.

In Mexico, this day is called *Candalaria*. To celebrate, a statue of the baby Jesus is dressed and lullabies are sung to him. In Argentina, a figure of the baby Jesus made of sugar is placed into a cake. All the children hope to find it in their piece when the cake is cut!

St. Valentine's Day (February 14). It is not clear how the customs connected with this day arose, nor exactly who St. Valentine was (several saints bear this name). There is a legend about one of these martyrs leaving a letter in his jail cell about his love and prayers for the daughter of the keeper of the prison.

You might want to adapt some of the current Valentine's Day traditions to make your celebration more Catholic. You could make and send cards with pictures of the Sacred Hearts of Jesus and Mary, for example, or tell the people you are close to how much they mean to you. Making a valentine for each person in your family or class can be a way to show that, for Christians, love is not exclusively romantic but includes everyone.

St. Valentine's Day can be a good time for instructing the young on the true meaning of romantic love in the context of the vocation of marriage.

Chair of St. Peter (February 22). The feast of the Chair of St. Peter is celebrated as a sign of the unity of the Church founded upon this apostle. This is a good day for your family to discuss why Catholics believe that the Holy Father has a special grace from the Holy Spirit to teach in the Church on faith and morals in an infallible way.

MARCH

St. Patrick's Day (March 17). St. Patrick (390-461) was archbishop and apostle of Ireland. In the United States, at least, St. Patrick's Day has become a largely secular celebration. People wear bright green, have parades and parties, and enjoy Irish culture. Catholics should celebrate it too, but with a focus on gratitude for the tremendously graced efforts of St. Patrick in the evangelization of Ireland.

Here are some lines of a prayer by St. Patrick that you could say around the table, alternating speakers:

Christ with me, Christ before me
Christ behind me, Christ in me,
Christ beneath me, Christ above me,

Christ on my right, Christ on my left,
Christ where I lie, Christ where I sit,
Christ where I arise,
Christ in the heart of every man who thinks of me,
Christ in the mouth of every man who speaks of me,
Christ in every eye that sees me,
Christ in every ear that hears me,
Salvation is of the Lord,
Salvation is of Christ,
May your salvation, Lord be ever with us.[2]

St. Joseph, Husband of Mary (March 19). Although we know very little about St. Joseph, what we do know shows what extraordinary trust was placed in him as the guardian of Mary and Jesus. Because of his role in the holy family he is the patron of families. Outwardly there was nothing unusual about Joseph's daily life, and so many Catholics can identify with his ordinary labors as a carpenter and his devoted care for his family. We know that he was a strong man, a pure man, a prayerful man, and a wise one.

In San Juan Capistrano, California, St. Joseph's Day is when the swallows that have migrated south for the winter traditionally return to the Franciscan Mission church there. Many people come to the mission that day to see the swallows come back.

In Catholic Slovak families, St. Joseph's Day is traditionally celebrated with a big dinner, a special bread in the form of a cane or staff, and plays, singing, and dancing.

If you would like to do something special in your home for St. Joseph's Day, you can use this prayer service composed by Sr. Marsaia, a Franciscan nun.

Leader: The Lord sanctified him in his faith and meekness, and chose him out of all flesh.

All: God made him a father to the king and master of all his household.

Leader: He never doubted God's promise but was strengthened in his faith and gave glory to God.

All: Therefore through faith he was counted as justified.

Leader: Faith was at work in his deeds and by his deeds his faith became perfect.

All: The Lord is my helper and protector; he is my savior.

Leader: Glory to the Father and to the Son and to the Holy Spirit.

All: The Lord sanctified him in his faith and meekness, and chose him out of all flesh.

Reader: Joseph lived a life of obedience, without objection or complaint, full of living faith. We know of two great moments of trial, when he thought Mary might have been pregnant by another man and when he had to leave the land he knew to travel with the holy family to Egypt.

How faithful and obedient he was in following the leading of the angels. This obedience is not acquired in a crisis; it is the fruit of many years of fidelity. We, ourselves, cannot hope to be better in a crisis than we have trained ourselves to be in little things.

Scripture does not show God working miracles to save St. Joseph labor or trouble, or humble carefulness and foresight. He guarded and guided and blessed with success what St. Joseph did, but the success had to be worked for. In this his life was like ours. We must face the fact that God means to help us in our work, but not to free us from it.

Like St. Joseph, we are also called to live out our chaste love in lives of hidden devotion. Every life has a wellspring and a dignity from its love. Joseph's love was devoted to Jesus and Mary, God and the mother of God. His life, more truly than anyone else's, was "hidden with Christ in God." Why should not our inner life be like this? Centered on love, simple, devoted, personal for our Lord and his Mother.[3]

The Annunciation (March 25) is a celebration of the glorious moment when the Angel Gabriel came to announce to the Virgin Mary that she would conceive a child by the Holy Spirit, who would be the Savior of her people (Lk 1:26-38). It is lovely to light a candle before a favorite statue or picture of Mary and recite the Scripture about the Annunciation, perhaps having one person read the lines of the angel and another Mary's responses.

APRIL

St. Catherine of Siena (April 29). St. Catherine of Siena lived in the fourteenth century. She advised popes and rulers, wrote a profound work about her mystical experiences, and exerted great spiritual influence through her holiness and good works. Her feast is a good time to emphasize in your family or community group the great spiritual authority of women saints in the Church and the many roles they can play.

You can learn more about St. Catherine and other holy women in *Treasury of Women Saints,* by Ronda Chervin (Servant Publications).

MAY

May has long been considered the month of Mary and is celebrated with many customs and traditions. These are often not fixed for a particular day but vary according to local pastoral practice.

May customs in most Catholic parishes revolve around the crowning of Mary with flowers as queen of heaven and of our hearts. Girls and boys dress up in their first communion clothing or other nice garments and bring flowers in procession to an altar of Mary. Everyone sings hymns and often the congregation recites a litany to Mary. Sometimes this ceremony concludes with Benediction of the Blessed Sacrament and the Divine Praises. (Both these traditions are explained in chapter seven.)

In Catholic schools, such customs often take place during school time. Two children might be assigned to make a floral bouquet for the May crowning the next day. On one day in May, children have a half day of school, with the remaining time spent in church for Marian devotions, perhaps followed by games and a party in the parish hall.

In many parts of the world, Catholics pray the rosary more often during the month of May. In Uganda, groups of people congregate in a different home to pray the rosary each evening. During that time, small children kneel beside their parents and learn to pray the rosary by mimicking their example.

In the Philippines a custom called *Flores de Mayo*, or "Flowers of May," is celebrated throughout the month. All the children in catechism classes gather every afternoon—sorted by age and neighborhood—to have Bible study, games, and parties. They play games that test their knowledge of the catechism, and they gain points for right answers. At the end of May, the children receive rewards according to how many points they have acquired.

In Costa Rica, an image or statue of Mary is carried from house to house during May. A team brings the image to one home in the morning; it stays there all day and then is carried away at night after the rosary is prayed with the family. The same custom is observed in the Philippines, except that the statue stays a whole week in each house.

In Vietnam, May is a month of celebration—with flowers, folk dances, and rhythmic chants. The dancing is performed before or after the evening Mass by a troupe of twenty to thirty people. The dance troupes sometimes compete against one another.

St. Athanasius (May 2). St. Athanasius, who died in 373, was bishop of Alexandria in Egypt for many years. He fought against Arianism, a heresy that had swept through the Church. Exiled when his opponents were in ascendancy, he was later vindicated and became known as "the father of orthodoxy." The statement of faith called the Athanasian Creed was drawn from his writings.

You might use this feast as an opportunity to teach about this creed. At the same time it would be good to explain a church teaching called "baptism of desire." This form of baptism can be received by those who do not have access to the sacraments or perhaps even the teachings of the Church, but who long to believe and wish to fulfill God's will. Through the treasure of grace in the Church, God can save any person invincibly ignorant of the faith.

Vatican II upheld that we should concentrate on what our separated brethren of other Christian faiths share with us—rather than on what they do not.

Mother's Day (Second Sunday in May). Many parishes make special mention of mothers on this day. In some, each woman in the congregation receives a flower, with the priest pointing out that all women, whether biological mothers or not, have motherly hearts.

Family members can pray a blessing for mothers and grandmothers around the dining table on Mother's Day. Here is one:

God of love, listen to this prayer.
God of holy people, of Sarah, Ruth, and Rebekah;
God of holy Elizabeth, mother of John, of holy Mary, Mother of Jesus, bend down your ear to this request and bless the mother(s) of our family.
Bless her with the strength of your spirit, she who taught her children how to stand and how to walk.
Bless her with the melody of your love, she who has shared how to speak, how to sing and how to pray to you.
Bless her with a place at your eternal dinner table, she who has fed and nurtured the life that was formed within her while still helpless but embraced in her love.
Bless her today, now, in this lifetime, with good things,

with health. Bless her with joy, love, laughter and
pride with her child/children and surround her with
many good friends.

May she who carried life in her womb be carried one
day to your divine embrace, there, for all eternity, to
rejoice with her family and friends.

This blessing and all graces, we pray, descend upon the
mother of our family in the name of the Father, and
of the Son and of the Holy Spirit. Amen.

St. Isidore (May 15). St. Isidore is the patron saint of
farmers and gardeners, and also of the city of Madrid,
Spain. He lived in the twelfth century and worked as a
farm laborer on an estate near Madrid. He was married and had one son who died young. In the fields
after Mass, Isidore spent his time working on the land
and talking to God, his guardian angel, and the saints.
Other farm laborers and his employer thought he was
a phony. They liked to ridicule him—until they began
to see visions of angels helping him in his work.
Isidore was most generous in helping poorer people,
sometimes through the miraculous multiplication of
food. There were many miracles after his death as well.

In some regions ceremonies are held in the fields to
invoke Isidore's blessing on crops. You could arrange
to plant seeds or trees in your home garden on this
day and ask special blessings on these plants. Pray for
farmers and gardeners too.

Memorial Day (Last Monday in May). Many churches
have special Masses on this day, which is a national
holiday in the United States and commemorates those
who have died defending the country. It is a good

time to pray for veterans and their families and to pray for peace.

Feast of the Visitation (May 31). This celebrates Mary's visit to her cousin Elizabeth after Mary had learned she was going to be Jesus' mother. Arrange for a simple dramatic production, if possible, with one person being Mary and the other Elizabeth. Use the words from Scripture: Luke 1:39-55.

Invite Mary into your home as Elizabeth did, by making up your own prayer of welcome or reciting this one:

"Come, O Mary, come and live in this house. Give to each of us all the necessary spiritual graces just as you brought them to the house of Zachariah.... Be a light and joy for us as you were in the family of Nazareth. Increase our faith, our hope and charity."

JUNE

Charles Lwanga and Companions, Martyrs of Uganda (June 3). This African feast day is a public holiday. Three hundred thousand people or more come to the shrine of the martyrs each year. Some pilgrims come on foot from up to one hundred miles away, as a penance and to gain an indulgence.

You might want to have one person in the family read aloud from an account of the lives of these saints. Here is one:

The first Catholic missions were established in Uganda, Africa, in 1879 by the White Fathers. The first native ruler was friendly to the missionaries, but the next one, Mwanga, wanted to root out this new religion, especially because Saint Joseph Mkasa admonished him for his sinful homosexual practices and his massacre of Protestant missionaries.

When Christian boys in Mwanga's service refused to pander to his vices, he had St. Joseph Mkasa beheaded. Later Mwanga executed the Christian pages, all under twenty-five years of age, after marching them thirty-seven miles to their death. They went to their deaths full of youth and courage.

St. Anthony of Padua (June 13). St. Anthony (1195-1231) was a Franciscan preacher who was renowned for his eloquence and miracles. For obscure reasons, he is frequently invoked for the finding of lost objects. In Italy and in other countries where there are many Catholics of Italian origin, his feast day is celebrated with colorful processions and street fairs. The merriment and good food attract many people who are not Catholics into the streets to enjoy the festivities.

Father's Day (Third Sunday in June). A day for the entire family to go to Mass and pray for fathers and grandfathers. After a family meal, you might want to perform this simple ceremony: family members gather in a circle with father in the center; he lays hands in blessing over each child; then everyone prays over him.

St. Thomas More and St. John Fisher (June 22). These saints suffered martyrdom in London in June of 1535 because they defied the king of England by standing up for the authority of the pope.

Thomas More is one of the most popular of all lay saints. He was a lawyer, a literary figure, and a top government administrator. Many Catholics pray on this day for laymen, lawyers, writers, and government leaders, as well as for a spirit of obedience to the authority of the pope. The video *A Man For All Seasons,* about Thomas More, would be a good choice for family viewing on this day.

St. John Fisher was the only English bishop of his time to withstand all temptations and remain faithful to the pope. Catholics like to invoke his intercession for bishops.

Birth of St. John the Baptist (June 24). This feast celebrates the birth of John the Baptist described so memorably by St. Luke. Celebrate the day by reading out the full account from the first chapter of the Gospel.

In Hispanic and Italian cultures, a great deal of tradition surrounds this feast. There are hourly Masses, processions with statues of Mary and the saints, stalls for culinary treats, bands, speeches, and fireworks. In Mexico, people throw water at each other on this feast as a sign of baptism! If you live in a city where there is an Italian or Hispanic parish, you might want to start a custom of visiting that church and enjoying the fiesta spirit.

This feast might be a good time to start a list of the dates of the baptisms of each member of your extended family or group. Keep the list in view so that you can arrange little ceremonies with prayers and treats each year on these days.

JULY

St. Junipero Serra (July 1). This newly canonized Franciscan priest (1713-1784) was responsible for most of the missions that began the evangelization of California. You might want to get a children's book or video about Serra to celebrate his heroic deeds.

St. Thomas (July 3). This is the apostle Thomas, the famous "doubting Thomas" of the Bible. He was a Jew and probably a Galilean. His name means twin. He is supposed to have preached the gospel in India.

St. Benedict (July 11). The feast day of the founder of the Benedictine Order (480-547) is celebrated with joy at the many Benedictine monasteries around the world by monks and nuns of the order and also by Oblates, lay people who are bonded to the monastery by prayer and mutual support.

It is largely due to the Benedictine tradition in the Church that the Liturgy of the Hours—especially in its sung form—has become part of our universal heritage. This feast, therefore, might be the moment to introduce your family or group to this form of prayer. Buy a book that contains the morning, evening, and night prayers at least, and begin praying one or more of these hours together. This may be confusing at first, so ask for help if you need it. Any priest, brother, or sister can teach you. (More on the Liturgy of the Hours in chapter seven.)

Lovers of classical music enjoy listening to the Liturgy of the Hours sung in Gregorian chant. Many beautiful recordings of these prayers are available on tape or compact disc for use at home or in the car.

Blessed Kateri Tekakwitha (July 14). Our first Native American saint, Kateri was born in what is today Auriesville, New York, in 1656. When the smallpox epidemic took her mother, father, and brother, she was adopted by relatives. Jesuit missionaries converted and baptized Kateri in 1676. Much persecuted by her Indian kinsmen, she fled to the mission in Montreal. There she took a vow of perpetual virginity in 1679 and died shortly afterward. She was beatified for her great charity to the poor and sick.[4]

Our Lady of Mount Carmel (July 16). In thirteenth-century England there lived a man of great wisdom and holiness named Simon Stock. He was the general of the Carmelite order. The Blessed Virgin came to him and gave him a scapular. (See chapter seven for an explanation of scapulars.) She told him it was a special sign of her love and that whoever died wearing it would be saved from hell. All those who wore the scapular out of love for her would enjoy her protection, she said, and would be released promptly from purgatory, on the first Saturday after their death.

One way to celebrate this feast is to obtain and begin to wear these brown scapulars. You can find them at Catholic religious goods stores.

Another way to celebrate is by reading from the writings of the most famous Carmelite saints: Teresa of Avila, John of the Cross, and Thérèse of Lisieux. You might read selected passages on their feast days, as well as on this one.

The Carmelite orders of nuns, priests, brothers, and secular Carmelites (lay people who participate in the charisms and graces of the order) are strong on contemplative prayer: opening oneself to quiet communion with the Lord with an emphasis on giving him space to initiate grace in one's soul. They also focus on offering sufferings in reparation for their own and others' sins. You might consider imitating these practices; they are of great worth for all Christians, whether formally joined to the Carmelite orders or not.

St. Mary Magdalene (July 22). The feast of St. Mary Magdalene is a good time to insure that everyone in the family realizes that even public sinners can become great saints. You might read the following scripture passage, which has traditionally been applied to Mary Magdalene:

> One of the Pharisees asked Jesus to eat with him, and he went into the Pharisee's house and took his place at the table. And a woman in the city, who was a sinner, having learned that he was eating in the Pharisee's house, brought an alabaster jar of ointment. She stood behind him at his feet, weeping, and began to bathe his feet with her tears and to dry them with her hair. Then she continued kissing his feet and anointing them with the ointment.
>
> Now when the Pharisee who had invited him saw it, he said to himself, "If this man were a prophet, he would have known who and what kind of woman this is and who is touching him—that she is a sinner."
>
> Jesus spoke up and said to him, "Simon, I have something to say to you."

"Teacher," he replied, "speak."

"A certain creditor had two debtors; one owed five hundred denarii, and the other fifty. When they could not pay, he canceled the debts for both of them. Now which of them will love him more?"

Simon answered, "I suppose the one for whom he canceled the greater debt."

And Jesus said to him, "You have judged rightly." Then turning toward the woman, he said to Simon, "Do you see this woman? I entered your house, you gave me no water for my feet, but she has bathed my feet with her tears and dried them with her hair. You gave me no kiss, but from the time I came in she has not stopped kissing my feet. You did not anoint my head with oil, but she has anointed my feet with ointment. Therefore, I tell you, her sins, which were many, have been forgiven; hence she has shown great love. But the one to whom little is forgiven, loves little." Then he said to her, "Your sins are forgiven…. your faith has saved you; go in peace."

LUKE 7:36-50

St. Ignatius Loyola (July 31). The founder of the Jesuit order, St. Ignatius (1491-1556) is known for the retreats he developed not only for consecrated religious but also for lay people. His retreats involve a program of "spiritual exercises." These meditations may be used either on long, private retreats of eight or thirty days or at home, as a series of exercises to do over a few months at home for an hour and a half a day. (For more on retreats, see chapter seven.)

AUGUST

Feast of the Transfiguration (August 6). This feast day commemorates the beautiful experience recorded in Matthew 17, Mark 9, and Luke 9: Jesus chooses three disciples—Peter, James, and John—to go and pray with him on the top of a mountain; he becomes radiant with glory.

You might read these Gospel accounts during your family or group prayer. Have members of your household act out the different roles described in these Gospels.

In the Eastern rites of the Catholic Church, members of the congregation bring large bowls of fruit to church to be blessed on the feast of the Transfiguration. The fruit symbolizes what happened to the apostles at the Transfiguration: the Holy Spirit became present to them, and this event contained the seeds that would ripen into the fruits of the Spirit within all Christians throughout time. After the blessing, the fruit is brought home to share with family and neighbors.

St. Dominic (August 8). St. Dominic was born in Castile, Spain, in 1170. A passionate preacher, he founded the Dominican Order of Preachers devoted to teaching Catholic truth and combating the heresies of the time.

Because the Dominican Order is known for its preaching, this feast is a good day to pray for all preachers. It is also an appropriate time to ask the Holy Spirit for help to overcome shyness about evangelizing the people we meet at school, at work, and elsewhere.

The Assumption of Our Lady (August 15). Because Mary was conceived without original sin, she did not inherit the type of bodily death the rest of us did. It is a dogma of the Catholic Church that Mary's body was assumed—taken up—into heaven.

The feast of the Assumption is a wonderful day to reflect on what our own resurrected bodies will be like—without any defects, able to move swiftly, a perfect expression of the beauty of our redeemed souls. In a group, members could share what, in their present experiences, gives them the most glorious image of what the resurrected body could be like (such as watching dancers, diving, the closeness of friends at a gathering).

The Dormition of Mary is celebrated in the Eastern rites of Catholic churches on August 15; it is given even more prominence than is the Assumption in the Western rite. The feast day is preceded by a fast that begins on the first of August. On the feast day itself, people bring herbal plants and flowers to church to be blessed and then take them home to be planted. This recalls the legend that when the early Christians looked at Mary's body in the grave where they had placed her, they found only flowers and herbs.

Queenship of Mary (August 22). Most older Catholics will be familiar with the melody to the famous hymn, "Hail Holy Queen." It can be found in most hymnals. Sing or pray it on this day:

"Hail! Holy Queen, Mother of Mercy. Hail, our life, our sweetness and our hope. To thee do we cry, poor banished children of Eve; to thee do we send up our sighs, mourning and weeping in this vale of tears. Turn then,

> *most gracious advocate, thine eyes of mercy toward us;*
> *and after this our exile, show unto us the blessed fruit of*
> *thy womb, Jesus. O clement, O loving, O sweet Virgin*
> *Mary! Pray for us, O holy Mother of God. That we may*
> *be made worthy of the promises of Christ."* [5]

St. Augustine (August 28). Saint Augustine was a fourth-century saint who began as one of the most famous of sinners. His mother, St. Monica, was Catholic but his father was pagan.

He spent his youth trying to evade education and amusing himself with a gang of teenagers in lustful and thieving activities. For this reason he makes an excellent patron for "bad boys," for God did not leave him in this condition. After a stormy young adulthood, Augustine was baptized a Catholic and became not only a holy priest but also a fine bishop. His beautiful and profound writings won him a place among the Doctors of the Church. *The Confessions*, Augustine's account of his journey to salvation, is a spiritual classic.

The feast of St. Augustine is a day when many Catholics feel inspired to pray for the grace to overcome the temptations that ensnare them most—a time to open themselves more to God's healing graces through means such as confession, counseling, or Twelve-Step programs.

SEPTEMBER

Birth of Mary (September 8). This day is traditionally celebrated as Mary's birthday, so bring a statue of Mary into your prayer area and have the younger children sing "Happy Birthday" to her. Praying the joyful mysteries of the rosary together is also a good way to celebrate our mother in heaven.

Triumph of the Cross (September 14). This celebration comes from a tradition about St. Helena, the mother of the emperor Constantine. She is said to have gone to Jerusalem in the early part of the fourth century to find the true cross on which our Savior died. When three crosses were found buried near the supposed site of Christ's death, the sick were brought near to each of them. Many were miraculously healed upon touching one of the crosses, which was then proclaimed the true cross.

Later Constantine erected the Church of the Holy Sepulcher on that spot.

Our Lady of Sorrows (Sept 15). This is a good day to pray the sorrowful mysteries of the rosary together with the family or community. (See chapter seven for a description of this Marian devotion.)

In Mexico, some families have a statue of Our Lady of Sorrows, *Altar de Dolores*, in their homes. In front of this statue they place pots with growing grass and beautiful jars with colored water.

Our Lady of Sorrows is the patroness of the Slovak people. She is honored by a novena leading up to her feast day.

Feast of the Korean Martyrs (Sept 20). During the eighteenth century some Chinese Christian books were brought into Korea. When a Chinese priest came to Korea years later he found four thousand Christians waiting for him. After he was killed, the Korean Catholics lived without a priest for thirty years. In 1837 Father Laurence Imbert, a missionary from France, came to Korea in disguise, along with some other priests. They organized an underground church. In less than two years there were nine thousand Korean Catholics. The relics of eighty-one martyrs of the Korean church are venerated (when possible, they are carried into the church at Mass in a reliquary) and the beatified leaders are celebrated on this day.

St. Matthew (Sept 21). St. Matthew was one of the twelve apostles and has traditionally been considered the author of the first Gospel. At the time of Jesus, tax collectors like Matthew were much hated by the people, since they charged over and above the already high Roman taxes to augment their own incomes. Nonetheless, Jesus chose Matthew and this saint-to-be immediately left his toll booth to follow the Lord.

You might like to read Matthew 9:9-13 about the calling of the apostle and also pray for all those in our times who are involved in business matters that are oppressive to others.

St. Vincent de Paul (September 27). St. Vincent de Paul was a French saint of the seventeenth century who founded a congregation of priests and a religious order, the Daughters of Charity, to take care of the needs of the poorest of the poor. Years later, in 1833, a French student named Frederic Ozanam founded a society to alleviate the sufferings of the poor; he named it after St. Vincent. (Ozanam was beatified in 1993.)

Nowadays, this St. Vincent de Paul Society maintains centers and thrift shops in many cities of the world and provides aid to the poor and homeless. Its large bins for the deposit of used clothing can be seen on the grounds of many parishes.

In some families St. Vincent's feast day is a time to clean out closets and donate serviceable clothing and other items to the poor.

Archangels Michael, Gabriel, and Raphael (September 29). These three angels are mentioned by name in Scripture. Michael is the most prominent angel in the Book of Revelation; Gabriel is the angel of the Annunciation in the Gospel of Luke; in the Book of Tobit, Raphael is sent by God to guide the young Tobiah on a journey that will bring healing to Tobit.

Michael is especially invoked as a defense against the wiles of the bad angels we call demons. You can pray the following prayer to him:

"Saint Michael, the Archangel, defend us in battle; be our protection against the wickedness and snares of the devil. May God rebuke him, we humbly pray, and do thou, O Prince of the Heavenly hosts, by the power of God, thrust into Hell Satan and the other evil spirits who prowl about the world seeking the ruin of souls. Amen." [6]

OCTOBER

St. Thérèse of Lisieux (October 1). One of the most popular saints of all times, St. Thérèse was born in France in 1873. She lived a short, hidden life as a Carmelite nun (she died in 1897), but her autobiography has made her beloved throughout the world. Today almost every church has its statue of little Thérèse.

What endeared this saint to so many Catholics is what she called her "little way" to God: offering every moment of one's life with great love to Jesus—even in the most ordinary of occupations, such as doing the laundry.

During her life Thérèse promised that she would continue to work for souls even after she went to heaven and that she would send roses to earth as a sign of this. In fact, there are many miracles attributed to St. Thérèse because flowers seem to accompany them in ways that cannot be explained by nature.

It is customary in some countries to eat chocolate eclairs on this day because Thérèse once said that these were one of her favorite treats.

Feast of the Guardian Angels (October 2). This feast day is a good time to commend each person in the family or community once again to the protection of his or her guardian angel. Children like to say this prayer:

"Angel of God, my guardian dear, to whom God's love commits me here, ever this day be at my side to light and guard, to rule and guide. Amen."

St. Francis of Assisi (October 4). Especially loved because of his spontaneous and joyful approach to prayer, St. Francis especially delighted in praising God in his creation. His feast day is a good time to recite his famous "Canticle of Brother Sun."[7] Here are some of the most beloved lines from this prayer:

Praised be you, my Lord, with all your creatures,
Especially Sir Brother Sun,
Who is daylight, and by him You shed light on us.
And he is beautiful and radiant with great splendor;
Of You, Most High, he is a symbol.

Be praised, my Lord, for Sister Moon
And the Stars.
In heaven You have formed them clear and
*   bright and fair.*

Be praised, my Lord, for Sister Water,
For she is very useful, humble, precious and pure.

Be praised, my Lord, for Brother Fire,
By whom You light up the night
For he is fair and merry and mighty and strong.

Be praised, my Lord, for our sister Mother Earth,
Who sustains and rules us,
And produces varied fruits with many-colored flowers
*   and plants.*

Praise and bless my Lord
And give Him thanks
And serve Him with great humility.

Because St. Francis was known for his love of animals, some churches have instituted a rite for the blessing of pets on his feast. There have even been blessings for large circus animals on this day. If no church near you holds such a service, bless your pets with holy water.

Our Lady of the Rosary (October 7). This feast commemorates an important naval victory won by the Christian fleet at Lepanto in 1571—a victory attributed to Mary's help invoked through the rosary.

Catholics celebrate the whole month of October as a special time for praying the rosary. Many pray it alone while driving, before bed, or as they fall asleep. But many Catholics also pray the rosary out loud with others—in church after daily Mass, in the family each evening, or on special feasts such as this one.

You can celebrate the feast of Our Lady of the Rosary by gathering the family or group to pray the rosary together—one decade for very small children, more for older members. (See "rosary" in chapter seven for more information about how to say this powerful prayer.)

You can also create a rosary book with young children which will help them to remember the mysteries of the rosary. Instructions for this project are at the end of this chapter.

St. Teresa of Avila (October 15). This sixteenth-century Spanish saint, the great reformer of the Carmelite order, is—along with Catherine of Siena—one of the two female Doctors of the Church. For this reason many statues show her with a pen and a paper. Her autobiography and other spiritual writings are loved for their chatty conversational style, pungency of wit, and sublimity of mystical union with Christ. You might celebrate her feast by having a member of the family or group read a selection from her writings.

St. Luke (October 18). St. Luke is mentioned in the Bible as a physician and a helper of St. Paul. Himself a gentile, Luke wrote his Gospel for other gentiles; it fills in many details not mentioned in the other Gospels, which were directed to Jewish readers. St. Luke also wrote the Acts of the Apostles.

A family or community might spend some days before or after this feast day reading Acts and discussing how it applies to their lives.

Isaac Jogues and other North American Martyrs (October 19). Among the missionaries who preached the gospel to the Indians in the United States and Canada are these French Jesuits who were martyred in the seventeenth century: Isaac Jogues, John de Brebeuf, Charles Garnier, Anthony Daniel, Gabriel Lallemant, Noel Chabanel, John Lalande, and Rene Goupil. They were canonized in 1930 by Pope Pius XI.

You might pray to them especially before the family meal. Ask them to intercede for the evangelization of the North American peoples of our time who have lost the faith or know it only partially.

St. Jude (October 28). St. Jude was the brother of St. James the Less and a relative of Jesus. For reasons which are not clear, he has been dubbed the "saint of the impossible," and many Catholics invoke his intercession for intentions that seem too difficult to come true.

St. Jude is particularly honored in India, where many novenas are said invoking his intercession. In Uganda too, three novenas are said at his shrine each year, drawing people from all over the country.

NOVEMBER

All Saints (November 1, day of obligation). This is a good day to find or buy books about the saints. Have each member of the family or community read up on a saint—his or her patron perhaps—and share this information with the others. If you have statues or pictures of the saints, assemble them in your devotional area.

Catholic religious goods stores usually carry a selection of such pictures and statues. Ceramic plaques of many saints can be obtained from St. Andrew's Abbey in California.[8]

In many European countries church sculptures and wayside shrines focus attention on the saints in colorful ways that stimulate the imagination. For example, St. Nepomajuk presides over a bridge in Eichstaett, Czechoslovakia: he was thrown into the river for refusing to reveal the sins he had been told in the confessional.

A similar effect is experienced in churches in Mexico, Central America, and South America. One of their charming and colorful customs is to dress statues in cloth garments. This gives them a certain warm realism.

In some Catholic schools on this feast, the children dress up as saints and process within the church or around the neighborhood. A litany of the saints is sometimes chanted using the names of the saints represented by the children in the procession.

All Souls (November 2). On this day, the Church prays for all those who have gone before us in death, and each of us prays especially that day and during the month for our own beloved dead.

What a consolation it is to ponder the Catholic doctrine of purgatory. We can hope that all these souls are being purified and prepared for complete union with God in heaven! In some churches (and families as well), it is customary to keep a beautiful book with parchment pages on which are written the names of the deceased and the dates of their death. This is displayed on a lectern during the month of November so that people passing by will remember to pray for the dead. In one parish the names of those who died during the year were written on a huge scroll and hung from above the altar.

In Germany, it is customary to take half a day off work on All Souls. People bring new flowers to the cemetery and put them on the graves of loved ones.

Probably the most famous All Souls Day traditions are those celebrated in Mexico for *Dia de los Muertos*, the Day of the Dead. A Mexican professor told me that while these customs may seem morbid to spectators from other countries, Mexicans love this day which shows that we can laugh at death.

The day is celebrated like a carnival. There are good things to eat, like skulls with your name on them made of sugar, and round bread topped with bones made of sugar. There are also fun things to do—watching skeleton puppets cavort on a stage, and playing with a clay tomb that has tiny figures of a priest and altar boys on it.

More soberly, people go to the cemetery and bring flowers to their dead and pray for good things for the future. Of course, Masses are said for the dead, with many candles and lots of incense. On this day a bright yellow-orange flower called the flower of death is predominant.

St. Martin de Porres (November 3). This Peruvian saint (315-397) of mixed ancestry (Spanish and Panamanian), born out of wedlock, is especially revered by

African American and Hispanic Catholics. His feast day might be a time for special prayers for single parents and their children.

St. Frances Cabrini (November 13). St. Frances Cabrini is one of the saints we especially honor in the United States. She came from Italy to our country at the end of the nineteenth century in order to minister to immigrants who had no one to teach them in their own tongue. She was the foundress of the Missionary Sisters of the Sacred Heart and established many schools, hospitals, and orphanages. You might use this day to pray for a beloved nun of your acquaintance.

St. Gertrude (November 16). St. Gertrude was a thirteenth-century Benedictine nun who had many dialogues with Christ. In one of them, Our Lord told her that the following prayer would release one thousand souls from purgatory each time it is said:

"Eternal Father, I offer thee the most precious blood of thy divine Son, Jesus, in union with the Masses said throughout the world today, for all the holy souls in purgatory, for sinners everywhere, for sinners in the universal church, those in my own home and within my family. Amen."

Some Catholics pray this prayer on the feast of St. Gertrude and also on All Souls, Good Friday, and at other times such as anniversaries of the death of relatives and friends.

Thanksgiving (Fourth Thursday in November). Many Catholic families go to Mass on Thanksgiving. After all, "Eucharist" *means* thanksgiving.

At dinner time, have each person at the table thank God aloud for some blessing of the year. At the end of the meal, after the smaller children are dispersed, you may want to add some prayers from the liturgy of the day:

"... Sing psalms and hymns and spiritual songs among yourselves, singing and making melody to the Lord in your hearts, giving thanks to God the Father at all times and for everything in the name of our Lord Jesus Christ." EPHESIANS 5:19-20

Father, all-powerful, your gifts of love are countless and your goodness infinite. On Thanksgiving Day we come before you with gratitude for your kindness: open our hearts to concern for our fellow men and women, so that we may share your gifts in loving service. We ask this through our Lord Jesus Christ, your Son, who lives and reigns with you and the Holy Spirit, one God, forever and ever. Amen.

St. Catherine Laboure (November 28). In 1830, Our Lady appeared to this French nun in her convent in Paris. While Catherine was in bed, she was awakened by a child clothed in white who told her to come to the chapel to see Mary. There she saw Our Lady seated in a chair. Catherine flung herself toward Mary and rested her hands in her lap.

In the course of several such visions, Catherine was told to have a medal made with a picture of Mary on it and a prayer. This medal, called the Miraculous Medal, was spread around the whole world.

The feast of St. Catherine Laboure might be a good time to get these medals for your family. (They can be obtained very inexpensively.) Mary promised that those who wear her medal and pray to her will receive special blessings.[9]

December

St. Barbara's Day (December 4). St. Barbara has been the subject of many legends. She is supposed to have been brought before a judge and tortured at the request of her father, who then cut off her head himself. (He was promptly punished by a lightning bolt, which killed him.) St. Barbara is traditionally invoked to aid in any sort of bad weather, even the emotional kind. For some reason, unmarried young women also turn to her for help in finding a husband.

In Austria, there is a custom called "cutting the cherry twigs" on Saint Barbara's Day. Anyone who is not married cuts a twig from a cherry tree and puts it in water. If the twig blossoms on Christmas Day, she will supposedly be married within the year.

In Lebanon, some of the stories about this fourth-century martyr are enacted on this day. To the beating of a drum and singing and dancing, Barbara's father, a pagan king, appears to seize his daughter. Barbara escapes. The soldiers come for her too, but she changes her clothes and escapes in disguise. As part of this story the saint is said to have hidden herself in a wheat field, where God made the wheat grow tall enough to conceal her; the Lebanese commemorate this incident by eating wheat soup on this day.

St. Nicholas' Day (December 6). St. Nicholas was the bishop of Myra, in Turkey, in the fourth century. In this role, he is supposed to have helped the poor by doing things like secretively hurling bags of money into their windows. He is the historical figure behind Santa Claus, loved by children the world over. Each year on this day Dutch families "welcome" St. Nicholas (*Sinter Klaas*) and his assistant, Black Peter (both figures are family members dressed in costumes), into their homes and exchange presents with original poems attached to them.

Immaculate Conception (December 8, day of obligation). Many Catholics misunderstand the meaning of this feast. It refers to the dogma that Mary had no original sin even though her conception took place in a natural manner. Some follow the custom of praying the Little Office of the Immaculate Conception on this day.[10]

Our Lady of Guadalupe (December 12). In the sixteenth century when the Spanish Catholics came to Mexico, the work of the missionaries was impeded by the evil deeds of the greedy, violent colonialists. Our Lady found a beautiful way to bring about huge numbers of conversions.

She appeared to a peasant, Juan Diego, as a pregnant Mexican woman and told him to go to the bishop and tell him to build her a shrine. The bishop was skeptical—until Juan Diego returned with two confirming signs: an image of the apparition reproduced on his cloak, and armfuls of roses that could not have grown naturally, as it was winter in the region.

Juan Diego's miraculous cloak is on display at the shrine of Our Lady of Guadalupe in Mexico City. Many Catholics make a pilgrimage there each year to see the mantle and to pray for special graces. With advanced techniques of photographic enlargement, some photographers maintain that you can also see the image of Juan Diego on the mantle, in the eyes of Our Lady.

In Hispanic parishes there is always a large picture of Our Lady of Guadalupe and it is carried on procession on her feast day. Sometimes too there is a little play depicting the famous scene where Juan Diego realizes that the image of the Virgin has been imprinted on his mantle.

St. Lucy (December 13). St. Lucy, or "Santa Lucia," is a Sicilian saint, another martyr of the early Church and the subject of many legends. She is said to have rejected an offer of marriage, upon which her suitor denounced her as a Christian. Ordered burned to death, Lucy was spared the flames and proclaimed that the power of the Lord had saved her. She was finally martyred by a sword to the throat.

In Norway and Sweden, there is an old custom where the oldest daughter of the family wears a crown of candles and serves a special cake to the family.

St. John the Evangelist (December 27). A way of celebrating the feast day of this great apostle and evangelist is to read the prologue to the Gospel of St. John and share your reflections about it.

New Year's Eve (December 31). In the early days of the Church, New Year's Eve was spent in prayer, partly to counteract the excesses of the pagans in what we would now call partying.

In our time, many Catholics and other Christians stay at home on this night of wildness. Or they get together with others for prayer, listening to religious music, and fellowship. This is also a good time to ask forgiveness for anything you have done to hurt someone in the past year.

One of Ronda's favorite New Year's Eve memories is a celebration in Austria. Families began by walking through the town and leaving candles at the graves of relatives. Then they proceeded to the houses of friends. The rooms were brightly lit; the tree with its Christmas decorations was still in place, as was the crèche. When the guests had arrived hot punch was served, and the musical members of the host family and their friends played a quintet, followed by choral singing. Then came chanting of night prayer, delicious foods, a prayer at midnight and the walk home through the snowy night.

In her book *The Year and Our Children* (New York: Image Books, 1964), Mary Reed Newland suggests a family celebration of the new year. (This suggestion works for other groups too.) Each person brings to the party a token of a blessing received during the past year: perhaps a doll to signify a new baby, or a picture of a car to represent that new vehicle, or candy hearts for new friends. These tokens are assembled around a table and the group guesses whose they are and what they represent, with everyone saying "Thank you, God."

∼ *For Your Home* ∼

Start a Eucharistic home shrine. Corpus Christi is a good day to encourage a family tradition of adoring Jesus in the Eucharist. One way to do this is through the Eucharistic Home Shrine movement, now known on seven continents.[11] A family or community sets up a Eucharistic home shrine by putting up a special picture, designed by the founder of the movement to inspire thanksgiving and reparation to the Eucharistic Heart of Jesus and the Sorrowful and Immaculate Heart of Mary.

This picture reminds everyone that the Lord loves them and awaits them in the Eucharist and wishes them to respond by frequent reception of Holy Communion. At each Mass, members of the Home Eucharistic Shrine group pray that Christ would visit all the home shrines in a special way and bless everyone in the family or group.

Create your own rosary book! Collect old pictures from religious calendars, Christmas cards, or other sources. You will also need a photo album, construction paper, and other art supplies such as crayons, markers, scissors, and paste.

Gather your children together and briefly explain the project. At this time, don't go into any lengthy descriptions of the rosary, so as not to lose your audience! Simply explain that the rosary is divided into mysteries, and they should choose pictures which best reflect the meaning of the mysteries to them.

Depending on how your children work best, you can assign different mysteries to each child or have them work together as a team. Explain that if they prefer, they can draw their own pictures.

When the children have finished, organize the pictures in order in the photo album.

Explain the meaning of the first mystery. Give the child or children who created this page a chance to explain what the picture means. Continue until all the mysteries have been discussed.

Now you can use this book whenever you say the rosary with your children.

CHAPTER 7

CUSTOMS AND TRADITIONS FOR THE WHOLE YEAR

A

Acts of Faith, Hope and Love. It is a tradition among Catholics to interrupt dismal trains of thought by lifting up the heart in prayers called acts of faith, hope, and love. Here are some forms for such acts:

Act of Faith: *"O my God, I firmly believe that you are one God in three divine persons, Father, Son, and Holy Spirit. I believe that your divine Son became man, died for our sins, and that he will come to judge the living and the dead. I believe these and all the truths which the holy Catholic Church teaches, because you have revealed them, who can neither deceive nor be deceived."*

Act of Hope: *"O my God, relying on your almighty power and infinite mercy and promises, I hope to obtain pardon of my sins, the help of your grace, and life ever-*

lasting through the merits of Jesus Christ, my Lord and Redeemer."

Act of Love: *"O my God, I love you above all things, with my whole heart and soul, because you are all-good and worthy of all love. I love my neighbor as myself for the love of you. I forgive all who have injured me, and ask pardon of all whom I have injured. Amen."*

The Angelus. This prayer is traditionally said three times a day—at six in the morning, noon, and six in the evening—to commemorate the Incarnation. It is a much-loved way to remember to whom we belong and to what we aspire as Catholics in the very midst of the daily routines of life and work that tend to distract us. The prayer is designed to be said by one person or responsorially in a group (group responses are noted in bold type).[1]

The Angel of the Lord declared unto Mary:
And she conceived of the Holy Spirit.
   Hail Mary...
Behold the handmaid of the Lord:
Be it done unto me according to your word.
   Hail Mary...
And the Word was made flesh:
And dwelt among us. Hail Mary...
Pray for us, O holy Mother of God.
That we may be made worthy of the
   promises of Christ.

Let us pray: Pour forth, we beseech you, O Lord, your grace into our hearts; that as we have known the incarnation of Christ, your Son by the message of an angel, so

*by his passion and cross we may be brought to the glory
of his resurrection. Through the same Christ, our Lord.*
Amen.

B

Banners, posters, and wall hangings. Some artistic
Catholics like to spend time working on banners and
posters for use in the church and at home. Such art
work has become popular, especially because of the
relatively low cost of the materials needed.

Christian homes often have wall decorations of
small, embroidered cloths framed in wood with say-
ings from Scripture or quotations from the saints. In
Latino cultures, one can often find rug-size renditions
of holy themes such as the Last Supper displayed on
the walls.

Bedtime prayer. It is a time-honored custom for
Catholics to end the day with a prayer of their choice
including elements of contrition for the sins of the day,
forgiveness of others, praying for special intentions and
asking God's protection for the night. In the past
almost all Catholics said such prayers on their knees.
Nowadays this varies from culture to culture.

In Vietnam many Catholics pray every night before
bed as a family, spending about thirty minutes between the rosary and the litany of the saints.

Benediction of the Blessed Sacrament. This is a short
service that includes prayers, a Eucharistic hymn, and
the blessing of the congregation with the Blessed Sacra-

ment. Although Benediction takes place in church rather than the home, we are including it here because families often decide to attend it together. If Benediction is offered in your church every week or from time to time on special feast days, you might want to make a decision to go together as a family or group. A treat afterwards for children can increase their willingness to attend!

Bible reading. All members of the family who are old enough to read could benefit from reading Scripture each day. A practice of some Catholics that will help children benefit from this is to insert one's own name into the passage wherever this is possible: "Ronda, I am the bread of life" or "Carla, do not fear. I am with you for all ages."

If Bible reading is being done together as a family or group, you can take turns reading a few verses, with the others giving their own reflections.

Blessings. There are formal priestly blessings such as the final blessing at the end of the Mass, or special prayers to bless holy objects like a crucifix or a statue.

In some Hispanic churches it is customary to have the priest bless your new car, and these blessings take place every weekend after the Masses. Having a new dwelling blessed is a custom for Catholics the world over and is usually done in a short formal ceremony by the priest. Various members of the family and group can be appointed to write or recite parts of such a service.

Many parents bless their children as they leave the house or go to bed by making the sign of the cross on the forehead, with or without the use of holy water or holy oil. Such a blessing is also customary before long or dangerous trips.

C

Candles. The use of holy candles is one of the most visible and prominent Catholic customs. Candles symbolize Jesus as the light of the world (Jn 8:12). It is a lovely tradition to keep the baptismal candle of each child, to be rekindled on his or her feast days and holidays such as Christmas and Easter.

Many Catholics like to light candles in church as a symbol of prayers offered for the dead or as an outward sign of prayers for any serious intention.

In many countries the use of vigil candles is a constant practice. Inexpensive little ones can be placed under holy pictures as a sign of veneration. Larger ones last many days and provide a soothing symbol of love for one who has died or for whose intention one is praying in a special way.

Catechetical study. Some Catholic homes keep a good catechism handy for reference and study. Good choices are the ones by Fr. John Hardon, S.J. such as *The Pocket Catholic Catechism*, or *The Faith*, and of course *The Catechism of the Catholic Church*. So often children and non-Catholics ask questions about doctrine or practice; it is helpful to have a definite answer.

Useful leaflets and other materials can be kept in the same place (for example, a list of the Ten Commandments that explains fully what falls under each one).

Confession. Canon law does not require confession, except for those in mortal sin. Many Catholics, however, make use of the sacrament of reconciliation as often as once a week, or at least once a year. By doing this, they avail themselves of the redemption Christ won for them on the cross, receive the healing graces he wants to offer through his priests, and receive strength to overcome sinful patterns in their lives.

Consecrations. There is a long tradition in the Catholic Church of consecrating oneself to Jesus or Mary under the name of some revelation, such as the Sacred Heart of Jesus or the Immaculate Heart of Mary. Here is one such consecration:

Jesus, we proclaim you enthrone you as Lord and
    Friend of our family!
Yes, Lord, we do want you to rule over our hearts and
    wills through your loving heart.
Share our everyday life, our joys and sorrows.
Be our well-beloved brother, our intimate friend!

Come, Lord Jesus, come!
Our hearts and home are open to you.
Stay with us, we need you.
Release in our home the power of your Spirit,
    the healer, the consoler.
Save our family from the evil forces seeking
    to destroy us.

Our Father in heaven
    take away our stony hearts and give us new hearts
    unselfish, generous, pure hearts, filled with love
    for you!

Heal our hurts, bind up our wounds, unite us in love.
May our love go beyond our home
    and inspire us to love those in need as Jesus loves us.

Lord Jesus, to your loving, glorified Heart,
    your wounded heart,
    we dedicate, we consecrate our weak, our
    selfish hearts.
We humbly acknowledge that without you
    we can do nothing, but with your help and your
    grace we can do all things:
    "even though we walk through the valley of the
    shadow of death, we fear no evil, for you are with
    us, your rod and staff, they comfort us."

Mary, Mother of the Church and our mother,
    help us to make our family truly a domestic church
    that is a community of love, a worshipping,
    praying family.

Good St. Joseph, head of the Holy Family,
    watch over us as you watched over Jesus
    and Mary at Nazareth.
Obtain for each of us that same loving trust
    in divine providence
    that sustained you in all your trials.

May the Lord bless us and keep us!
May his face shine upon us and be gracious to us!
May he look upon this family with kindness and give
    us peace!
And may Almighty God bless us, the Father, the Son,
    and the Holy Spirit. Amen.
Praise the Lord, now and forever. Amen! [2]

Contemplative prayer. Contemplative prayer is likely to enter into our daily lives when we lift our hearts to God with a minimum of words and allow his grace to permeate our minds, hearts, souls, and bodies. This can be accompanied by occasional reading of a spiritual book—just a few lines to move the mind away from distractions and back into focus—or by a slow praying of the rosary or Divine Mercy prayers. (See "Mercy Prayer" in this chapter.)

D

Death and dying prayers. Catholics bring a dying person to a priest or call a priest to the home or hospital for a final confession and an anointing. Many pray litanies of the saints at the bedside and keep vigil candles lit in the room.

After the death of a loved one, many Catholics pray the Psalms and Scripture passages from the Office for the Dead; this is the section of the Liturgy of the Hours which is designed as intercession for those who have died.

In some countries, black mourning clothing is worn for a week or even for many years by close family members. In others, dark clothing is worn to the funeral Mass but not afterwards. Men of the family or friends in some countries wear a black ribbon in the buttonhole or a black armband for a week or more.

It is traditional for Catholics to have a holy card made up with the name of the deceased, the birthday and day of death, a photograph if possible, and a verse from Scripture. Mourners who come to the funeral can take a card home and tuck it in their prayer books as a way to remember to pray for the beloved dead person.

Praying the rosary the evening before the funeral Mass is a Catholic custom in many lands. This is done at the funeral home, at the home of relatives, or in church.

After the funeral Mass, the casket is usually brought to a Catholic cemetery for burial. Masses are offered all through the year for those within the sacred grounds.

Recently, mostly because of the great expense of funeral arrangements, canon law has allowed cremation. Most Catholics still prefer the casket and burial in the ground, however—not only because tradition can be comforting, but also because there are no liturgical rites connected with cremation. Sending ashes out to sea may have lovely aesthetic connotations but deprives the dead person of the graces coming from the Masses said at Catholic cemeteries.

In the Eastern rites of the Catholic Church, there are special prayers beside the main church area where a large crucifix is hung. These are sung at the time of death, forty days later, and at the first-year anniversary. It is customary for mourners to pay their respects not only to the dead person but also formally to the family at the graveside.

After a death in our family, we play a great classical requiem such as Mozart's or Verdi's *Requiem* or Elgar's *Dream of Gerontius,* about the soul after death (based on the poem by John Henry Cardinal Newman).

The Irish organize a wake—a party where people gather before the funeral Mass to celebrate the life of the deceased with drinking, eating, and reminiscences about the beloved dead person.

In Vietnam it is customary to keep the body in the home for three days of prayer. During that time, the casket is open and the family prays the rosary over and over. The color for funerals is white. Simple funeral garments for the mourners are made of special cloth, and a hood is attached for close family members. The casket is carried to the church—but not by family members—and after the funeral Mass all process to the cemetery. For the whole first month after a death, the family prays the rosary for the soul of the dead person. After one hundred days they gather again to pray, and then again on the first anniversary of death. After three years, they say their last ceremonial family prayers.

In Uganda when someone dies, the body is kept at home. Relatives and neighbors come to stay the night, resting in sleeping bags on the floor around the fire.

In Mexico people also come and stay the night, praying around the body.

Deliverance prayers. The full rite of exorcism can only be administered by a priest with the special permission of the bishop. However, there are traditional prayers that lay people are permitted to use in any situation where they think there is a need to stand against oppressive evil spirits or harassing evil thoughts and images. Here is one approved deliverance prayer:

In the name of the Father and of the Son and of the Holy Ghost. Amen.

Glorious prince of the celestial host, St. Michael the Archangel, defend us in the conflict which we have to sustain "... against principalities and powers, against the rulers of the world of this darkness, against the spirits of wickedness in the high places" (Eph 6:12). Come to the rescue of men, whom God has created to his image and likeness, and whom he has redeemed at a great price from the tyranny of the devil.

It is thou whom holy Church venerates as her guardian and her protector, thou whom the Lord has charged to conduct redeemed souls to heaven. Pray, therefore, the God of peace to subdue Satan beneath our feet, that he may no longer retain men captive nor do injury to the Church.

Present our prayers to the Most High, that without delay they may draw his mercy down upon us. Seize "the dragon, the old serpent, which is the devil and Satan," bind him and cast him into the bottomless pit ... that he may no more seduce the nations" (Rv 20:2-3).[3]

The Divine Praises. This prayer is most commonly used in the month of May, during the Marian devotion, and traditionally concludes Benediction of the Blessed Sacrament.[4]

Blessed be God.
Blessed be his holy name.
Blessed be Jesus Christ, true God and true man.
Blessed be the name of Jesus.
Blessed be his most Sacred Heart.
Blessed be his most Precious Blood.
Blessed be Jesus in the most holy Sacrament of the altar.
Blessed be the Holy Spirit, the Paraclete.
Blessed be the great Mother of God, Mary most holy.
Blessed be her holy and Immaculate Conception.
Blessed be her glorious Assumption.

Blessed be the name of Mary, Virgin and Mother.
Blessed be St. Joseph, her most chaste spouse.
Blessed be God in his angels and in his saints.

Donations. Canon law requires Catholics to support their parish church in whatever way is possible, given their particular financial situations. Many Catholics also contribute money on a regular basis to various charitable works of their choice. In the past few decades, Catholics have been urged to copy the custom of some Protestants who tithe (give ten percent) of their gross income to their churches and to various charities.

E

Enthronement of the Sacred Heart. This is a devotional ceremony in which a large picture of the Sacred Heart is placed in a prominent spot in the home—a sign of trust in the loving protection of Jesus, and of desire to respond to his love. Hymns are sung and special prayers are said. It is desirable to have a priest preside, but an adult family member can lead the ceremony.

Examination of conscience. It is a long-standing custom of Catholics to include in personal night-time prayer an examination of conscience. This means prayerfully considering the thoughts, words, and deeds of the day and asking forgiveness of God for any wrongdoing. This is followed by considerations for improving the next day by more attentive prayer and self-knowledge.

F

Fasting and penance. Fasting—limiting our intake of food and drink—is a way to discipline our unruly desires and express our intention to turn more fully to God. The Church has established regulations about when Catholics must fast (unless there is a serious impediment): on Ash Wednesday, Good Friday, and for one hour before receiving Holy Communion. In the Eastern rites, fasting is more frequent, rigorous, and widespread. (More on fasting and abstinence in chapter four.)

In recent times the old Catholic custom of fasting in addition to the obligatory times—as penance for one's own sins and in reparation for the sins of others—has gained in popularity. This can be attributed to the effect of various messages from Our Lady—at Fatima, for example, and in her alleged apparitions at Medjugorje.

In addition to fasting, Catholics undertake other types of penance. In Ireland, it is a tradition for pilgrims to climb the mountain of St. Patrick on their knees; this is also done at the Mount of the Cross in Medjugorje. In Rome pilgrims of all nationalities crawl up the *Scala Sancta* on their knees; tradition has it that these "sacred steps" are a replica of the steps leading up to the throne of Pontius Pilate.

Feast days (personal). Besides the universal feast days that the whole Church celebrates, Catholics also have a longstanding custom of celebrating the days on which they were baptized or the feast day of their patron saint. Some families keep track of these dates by keeping a list or by marking them on a church calendar or in the Liturgy of the Hours book.

The celebration of these personal feast days might include a little party, flowers, or accompanying that person to Mass on that day. In some families, everyone attends Mass together on these special anniversaries, even those who normally attend only Sunday Mass. This excursion can be followed by pizza or some other treat.

First Fridays and Saturdays. In the revelation she received, St. Mary Margaret Alacoque was promised that those who receive Holy Communion in a state of grace on the first Friday of every month will be saved. (For a listing of all the promises, refer to the feast of the Sacred Heart in chapter six.)

Still more recently, a tradition has arisen of also receiving Holy Communion on the first Saturday of every month in response to a request and promise made by Our Lady of Fatima: "I promise to help at the hour of death, with graces needed for salvation, whoever, on the first Saturday of five consecutive months, shall confess and receive Holy Communion, recite five decades of the rosary, and keep my company for fifteen minutes, while meditating on the mysteries of the rosary with the intention of making reparation to my Immaculate Heart."

In Mexico it is the custom on First Fridays and First Saturdays for women and men to come to Mass and sit with a special group of devotees. The women wear beautiful old mantillas. All wear a wide red ribbon holding a holy medal on the back or a scapular bearing the picture of the Sacred Heart and the Immaculate Heart.

G

Grace. Throughout the centuries, Catholics have been saying a grace—prayer of gratitude—before meals, whether alone or together in groups. The most common such prayer runs like this:

> *"Bless us, O Lord, and these thy gifts which we are about to receive through thy bounty, through Christ Our Lord. Amen."*

In Ireland, it is the custom to add the following words to this basic prayer: "May the souls of the faithful departed rest in peace."

Here is a grace prayer used by the Magnificat Woman's Group in Phoenix. It is sung to the tune of "Edelweiss," made famous for Americans by its prominence in the musical *The Sound of Music:*

Bless our friends, bless our food, Come, O Lord, and be with us. May our talk glow with peace, may our lives be united.

Friendship and love, may it bloom and grow, bloom and grow forever, bless our friends, bless our lives, bless us now and forever.

H

Healing prayers. Belief that Christ the Healer lives still, even after the Ascension, has always been the faith of the Church. Healing oils have always been used by priests in the anointing of those close to death and as part of the rites of other sacraments. However, this truth is balanced by the teaching that we must always accompany every prayer by "thy will be done." In order to draw us closer to him, God allows sufferings of all kinds; they are a form of penance for our sins and something we can offer for the sins of others.

Not so much in the United States but in many Catholic countries, when people suffering from physical ills believe themselves to have been healed in a supernatural manner, they often leave something in church—next to a crucifix or the entombed relics of a saint—as a sign of this event. At the shrine of Our Lady of Lourdes, for example, many crutches, braces, and other items testify to the healing of their former owners.

In Italy, the most common manner of commemorating a physical cure is to buy a gold or silver model of the part of the body that has been healed, such as an arm or a leg; then this is attached to a velvet curtain draped behind the crucifix or statue. Sometimes children leave toys as a sign of their healing.

In the last twenty-five years, there has been a growing custom of prayers for healing among the laity. Such prayers include informal praying over others for relief from sickness and pain, but also more elaborate prayers for inner healing of the heart and for healing the family tree. Books containing such prayers can be found in most Catholic bookstores.

The healing of memories is based on the belief that Jesus is present to all times: past, present, and future. When we realize that he was present in the past at times of great hurt—though we may not have experienced his presence consciously at the time—this can help us receive the love he wants to give us in compensation for such hurts. The following sample "healing of memories" prayer will show you what is involved:

Jesus, lover of my heart, I invite you to show me how you were present in my past life. Perhaps my parents didn't want a child when I was conceived. Let me realize that you overcame all those obstacles because you wanted me to be. Show me the hurts in the lives of my parents that made them so afraid to have me....

In school I felt I didn't fit in. Let me catch a glimpse of you watching me, full of compassion. Fill my heart with a sense of your love for that little girl (or boy) I was, so that I may always reach out with your love to children I meet who feel awkward....

In the family, you can compose a healing prayer not only for living relatives but also for those of the past. This can be especially helpful for those people in your family tree whose lives may have been disordered.

Holding hands while praying. This custom arose after Vatican II during experiments with different forms of group prayer. By now, many, many Catholics pray this way during grace, during the Our Father at Mass, and during one-on-one or circle prayer with friends.

Holy cards. Ever since printing became relatively inexpensive, Catholics have made use of holy cards as bookmarks in their missals, Liturgy of the Hours, and other books. Some Catholics decorate their desks or office walls with holy cards, statues, and religious paintings. (When this custom was more prevalent, it used to be an instant way of finding out which co-workers were Catholic!)

As mentioned above (see "Death and Dying Prayers"), Catholics usually have such cards made up as a way of honoring the deceased and remembering to pray for them. Holy cards are also printed to mark other occasions—ordinations and special anniversaries, for instance.

Holy Communion. It is the practice of most Catholics not in a state of mortal sin to receive Holy Communion on Sundays and also on other days of the week, even daily. In situations where you wish you could be receiving but cannot, you can make an act of spiritual communion such as this one, attributed to St. Francis of Assisi:

"I believe that you, O Jesus, are in the most holy sacrament. I love you and desire you. Come into my heart. I embrace you. Oh, never leave me. May the burning and most sweet power of your love, O Lord Jesus Christ, I beseech you, absorb my mind that I may die through love of your love, who were graciously pleased to die through love of my love."

Holy medals. There are many kinds of holy medals that Catholics traditionally wear around their necks or on bracelets or keep in their pockets and purses as a sign of devotion or as a petition for intercession and protection. The most famous of these is the Miraculous Medal. (See the entry for November 28 in chapter six.) Other medals bear an image of the Sacred Heart, our Lady (as represented in an approved apparition), a saint, or the symbol of a Third Order (explained later in this chapter).

Holy oil. Priests and bishops make use of specially blessed oil in sacraments such as baptism, anointing of the sick, and ordination. Lay people can also use holy oil; some carry a small bottle of it to use for blessing themselves or others.

Holy water. Blessing oneself with holy water is suggested whenever danger threatens—fire, storms, and illness, for example. It can also be sprinkled in a room or on a person to dispel the devil.

Every Catholic church has holy water fonts near its entrance where visitors can bless themselves as they enter the sacred space of the church. The usual practice is to dip one's fingers into the water and to make the sign of the cross: "In the name of the Father, the Son, and the Holy Spirit." Another recommended prayer is "By this holy water and by your precious blood, wash away all my sins, O Lord." It is also traditional to pray for the souls in purgatory while blessing oneself with holy water.

It is a custom in some countries to put a small holy water font by the entrance to the family dwelling. The font is kept full of holy water, which can be obtained at church by asking the priest or by drawing the water from the special container for that purpose. Simple holy water fonts can be obtained at most Catholic religious goods stores or monastery shops. In European countries such fonts are often quite elaborate and beautiful.

It is a custom of pilgrims to Marian shrines to bring back little plastic or glass bottles of holy water (water from Lourdes is especially well-known). These bottles can be kept in your devotional area and used in cases of illness, for anointing and praying for healing.

Hymn singing. A beautiful way to lift your heart to God and to drive out the smog of depressing thoughts is to sing hymns at home or in the car or walking down the street. Many Christians start the day by singing along with musical tapes.

I

"I am a Catholic" Cards. Many Catholics carry a card in their wallet or affixed to the registration in their cars indicating that they are Catholic and wish a priest to be called in case of danger of death.

Icons. It is a universal custom in the Eastern rites of the Catholic Church to display icons in churches and homes. Icons differ from Western art works on the same themes in that they are supposed to be painted only by those who pray deeply about their work; the painting therefore becomes a fruit of contemplation to be venerated, rather than a work of art produced for aesthetic or commercial reasons.

Among Eastern rite Catholics, it is customary for every home to have icons in each main room of the house, with a small vigil candle always burning in front of them. These icons are meant to make more vivid to the faithful the truth that Christ is really present in their homes. Individual and family prayers are usually said in front of the icons.

Icons can be found in the entryways of some houses and are rotated according to the feast days that have just been celebrated. Noel Plourde, a mother and a counselor who belongs to St. Andrew's Orthodox

(Uniate) Church in California, tells me how much it means to her to bring icons whenever she has to travel for speaking engagements. Displaying her icons in a strange hotel room, lighting a candle, and chanting the prayers of the services helps her to feel Jesus with her and also to feel bonded with her church community. Noel Plourde also points out that the nature of Russian Orthodox chant is to evoke strong emotions and that these are encouraged, for instance, during chants for the deceased. As a psychologist, she thinks that such prayers are good for the release of emotions.

Indulgences. An indulgence is a remission of the temporal punishments for sins. In the early Church heavy penances, to be carried out over a specified period of time—going on a ten-day pilgrimage, for example—were given for some sins. Today, instead of such penances, one can say special "indulgence prayers" or fulfill the requirements for gaining an indulgence through some other pious practice, such as visiting a particular church and praying there.

As is often suggested on holy cards, indulgences can also be gained for the souls in purgatory. These usually mention a certain time period such as a thirty-day indulgence.

One of the prayers with the largest indulgence that has become a custom for many Catholics is very simple—make this act of faith, silently or in a whisper, whenever you see the priest elevate the Host: "My Lord and my God."

Another very popular and traditional prayer with indulgences attached to it is the *Anima Christi:* [5]

Soul of Christ, sanctify me.
Body of Christ, save me.
Blood of Christ, fill me.
Water from the side of Christ, wash me.
Passion of Christ, strengthen me.
O Good Jesus, hear me.
Within your wounds hide me.
Suffer me not to be separated from you.
From the malignant enemy, defend me.
In the hour of my death, call me.
And bid me come unto you.
That with your saints I may praise you
For ever and ever. Amen.

Intercessory prayer. A beautiful tradition of many Catholics is to say a quick prayer for everyone you see, whether known or stranger, or to pray especially for those you do not care for much. You can also make it a bedtime practice to go through a mental or written list of people and ask God to bless each one.

J

Journal writing as a form of prayerful reflection. Keeping diaries or journals does not necessarily spring from a religious motive, of course. However, quite a number of Catholics now keep a journal as a way of deepening their prayer life and relationship with God. Journal entries are usually put in the form of an address to God, as in:

"Dear Jesus, today I feel so depressed. Help me to reach out to you, the source of all my joy...."

K

Kitchen Madonnas. A Slovak custom is to have in the kitchen a prominent statue or icon of the Madonna as a way of inviting her to preside over the vital function of cooking.

L

Litanies. Litanies are prayers of petition whose form dates back to the early Church. They are especially used in Eastern rites and in processions. By A.D. 1601 some eighty litanies were in use in honor of different mysteries of the faith.

Many Catholics recite litany prayers in honor of Jesus, Mary, the Holy Spirit, and the saints. Here is a typical litany you might want to try on a daily or occasional basis. You can say litanies alone or with others, with the leader intoning the first part and the family or group chiming in on the response: "have mercy on us," or "save us," and so on.

Some Catholics find litanies especially comforting in times of distress, perhaps when they are too upset to compose their own prayers but want to lift their hearts to Christ. As with the rosary, the rhythm of the litany can rock you into a state of peace.

THE LITANY OF THE MOST PRECIOUS BLOOD
OF OUR LORD JESUS CHRIST

Lord, have mercy on us.
Christ, have mercy on us.
Lord, have mercy on us.

Christ, hear us.

Christ, graciously hear us.

God, the Father of heaven, have mercy on us.

God, the Son, Redeemer of the world, have mercy on us.

God, the Holy Spirit, have mercy on us.

Holy Trinity, One God, have mercy on us.

Blood of Christ, only-begotten Son of the eternal Father, save us.

Blood of Christ, Incarnate Word of God, save us.

Blood of Christ, of the new and eternal testament, save us.

Blood of Christ, falling upon the earth in the agony, save us.

Blood of Christ, shed profusely in the scourging, save us.

Blood of Christ, flowing forth in the crowning of thorns, save us.

Blood of Christ, poured out on the cross, save us.

Blood of Christ, price of our salvation, save us.

Blood of Christ, without which there is no forgiveness, save us.

Blood of Christ, Eucharistic drink and refreshment of souls, save us.

Blood of Christ, stream of mercy, save us.

Blood of Christ, victor over demons, save us.

Blood of Christ, courage of martyrs, save us.

Blood of Christ, strength of confessors, save us.

Blood of Christ, bringing forth virgins, save us.

Blood of Christ, help of those in peril, save us.

Blood of Christ, relief of the burdened, save us.

Blood of Christ, solace in sorrow, save us.

Blood of Christ, hope of the penitent, save us.

Blood of Christ, consolation of the dying, save us.

Blood of Christ, peace and tenderness of hearts, save us.
Blood of Christ, pledge of eternal life, save us.
Blood of Christ, freeing souls from purgatory, save us.
Blood of Christ, most worthy of all glory and honor,
*   save us.*

Lamb of God, who takest away the sins of the world,
*   spare us, O Lord.*
Lamb of God, who takest away the sins of the world, gra-
*   ciously hear us, O Lord.*
Lamb of God, who takest away the sins of the world,
*   have mercy on us.*

You have redeemed us, O Lord, in your Blood and made
*   us, for our God, a kingdom.*
Let us pray. Almighty and eternal God, you have
appointed Your only begotten Son the Redeemer of the
world, and willed to be appeased by his Blood. Grant,
we beg of you, that we may worthily adore this price of
our salvation, and through its power be safeguarded
from the evils of this present life, so that we may rejoice
in its fruits forever in heaven. Through the same Christ
our Lord. Amen.

Catholic stores usually have small inexpensive
leaflets with litanies so that you can buy a set for family
or group use.

Liturgy of the Hours. This is the official cycle of prayers
by which the Church praises God and sanctifies the day.
Besides the rosary, this is the most common prayer of
all Catholics and can be used by older children. It goes
back to early Christian times and echoes the traditional
psalm praying of the Jewish people.

The Liturgy of the Hours comprises a sequence of

psalms, scriptural and other readings, and hymns. It is divided by the hours of the day (morning, midmorning, evening, and night, for example), feast days of the year, and liturgical seasons. Priests and religious are obliged to pray these hours. Many lay people join them in this prayer of the universal Church, reading and meditating on the prayers alone or in a group throughout the day at set times.

M

Masses for special intentions. It is an old Catholic custom to have the priest say a special Mass for someone who has died. Sometimes a card is sent to the bereaved announcing that such a Mass has been said. People arrange for these Masses at the rectory, usually giving a small donation. Various monasteries support themselves partially on donations coming from requests to have Masses said for various intentions, and an elaborate card is sent to the beneficiaries.

Sometimes people request a "perpetual Mass" in which the order promises that its priests will say Masses for this intention until the end of time, or as long as the order exists. Learning that perpetual Masses will be said even after your own death for a beloved relative or friend can be quite a consoling gift.

In recent years this tradition is expanding to include requests for Masses on people's birthdays, anniversaries, or for intentions such as recovery from illness.

The Memorare. Besides the rosary, the *Memorare* is perhaps the most beloved of all prayers asking for

Mary's intercession. It is thought to date back to the twelfth century and is traditionally attributed to St. Bernard of Clairvaux.

I, Ronda, used to find it difficult to say this prayer because I thought that the message in it about no one ever being left unaided by Mary meant that praying to her had infallible results. Gradually I came to see what this means: you will be helped, but not necessarily in the way you would choose. A prayer to get a certain job might lead to your getting a different one that is better for you in the long run, or a prayer for healing might lead to your finding the ultimate healing of being taken out of this world into the arms of Jesus.

THE MEMORARE

Remember, O most loving virgin Mary,
that it is a thing unheard of
that anyone ever had recourse to your protection
implored your help or sought your intercession
and was left forsaken.
Filled therefore with confidence
I fly to you, O Mother, virgin of virgins,
to you I come, before you stand, a sorrowful sinner.
Despise not my words, O Mother of the Word,
but hear and grant my prayer. Amen.[6]

Meditative prayer. Meditation means reflecting or reading about some truth of our faith, often pausing to lift your heart to God. For example, reflecting on how Christ died for us, you might pause and pray "Thank you, Jesus, for dying for my sins."

It is a Catholic custom to spend some time each day (the amount of time varies) on meditation. If the meditation takes its source from the reading of Scripture or other spiritual books it is called *lectio divina.* Here a passage is read slowly and reflectively and is received as a personal message from God to the reader.

Sometimes God himself interrupts the practice of meditation, as it were, by filling the soul with such quiet or such illumination that there is no need to reflect or to read further.

The mercy prayer. Many Catholics like to pause between three and four in the afternoon to pray the chaplet of Divine Mercy, sometimes simply called the mercy prayer. (The origin of this devotion is recounted in chapter five, in the section on Mercy Sunday.) You will need rosary beads.

CHAPLET OF DIVINE MERCY

Begin with an Our Father, Hail Mary and Apostles' Creed.

Then on the "Our Father" beads pray:

"Eternal Father, I offer you the body and blood, soul and divinity of your dearly beloved Son, Our Lord Jesus Christ, in atonement for our sins and those of the whole world."

On the Hail Mary beads pray:

"For the sake of his sorrowful passion, have mercy on us and on the whole world."

When you have prayed the whole rosary, using these prayers, conclude the chaplet by praying three times:

"Holy God, Holy Mighty One, Holy Immortal One, have mercy on us and on the whole world."

The missal. The missal is a large single volume or several smaller volumes providing the readings for Masses throughout the year. It is a custom of some Catholics to read and meditate on these passages the night before Mass or in church before the service begins.

Morning offering. Most Catholics are taught to begin the day with a prayer offering the pains, frustrations, and joys of the day to God for the building up of his kingdom. Here is a typical morning offering prayer:

I offer You Jesus, all my prayers, works, and sufferings of this day, for the intentions of your Sacred Heart, in union with the holy sacrifice of the Mass throughout the world, in reparation for all my sins and for the intentions of our Holy Father for this month. Amen.

Eastern rite Catholics usually pray a liturgical morning prayer (Matins) as a form of offering the day to Christ. Since many of these congregations are rather small and their liturgies require the presence of a chorus to sing with the priest, they are not always able to offer a daily Mass, as we do in the Roman rite. Praying Matins is therefore a form of daily rededication.

The Mystical Mass Prayer. A custom growing in popularity now in the Church is to link up the intercessory prayers of Catholics to the Mass in the form of what is called the Mystical Mass Prayer by Father Luke Zimmer, SS.CC.[7] It is called mystical because it links the Catholic up to all the Masses of the world that day. In eternity the wishes of Jesus, Mary, and Joseph are the same. They are said here therefore to have one heart.

Eternal Father, we offer to You, through the Immaculate and Sorrowful Heart of Mary, in the Holy Spirit, the body, blood, soul, and divinity of Our Lord Jesus Christ, in union with each Mass celebrated today and every day until the end of time.

With Mother Mary, St. Joseph, each angel and saint in heaven, each soul in purgatory, each person in the Body of Christ and the family of God, we offer each act of love, adoration, praise and worship.

We offer each act of thanksgiving for blessings, graces, and gifts received.

We offer each act of reparation for sins that have been, are being, and will be committed until the end of time. And we offer each act of intercessory prayer.

We offer all these prayers in union with Jesus in each Mass celebrated throughout the world until the end of time.

We stand before you, Triune God, like the prodigal son asking to be accepted, like the publican asking for mercy and forgiveness, like the paralytic asking for healing and strength, and like the good thief asking for salvation.

We consecrate ourselves and all of creation to you.

Eternal Father, we ask you in the name of Jesus, through the power of his Precious Blood, through his death on the cross, through his resurrection and ascension, to send forth the Holy Spirit upon all mankind.

Holy Spirit, we ask for an outpouring of your graces, blessings and gifts upon those who do not believe, that they may believe; upon those who are doubtful or confused, that they may understand; upon those who are lukewarm or indifferent, that they may be transformed; upon those who are constantly living in the state of sin, that they may be converted; upon those who are weak, that they may be strengthened; upon those who are holy, that they may persevere.

We ask you to bless our Holy Father. Give him strength and health in mind, body, soul, and spirit. Bless his ministry and make it fruitful. Protect him from his enemies.

Bless each cardinal, bishop, priest, brother, sister, and all aspiring to the religious life, especially.... and grant many the gift of a vocation to the priesthood and religious life.

Bless each member of our families, relatives and friends, especially....

Bless the poor, the sick, the underprivileged, the dying and all those in need....

Bless those who have died and are in the state of purification, that they may be taken to heaven....

We consecrate ourselves and all creation to you. Heart of Jesus, Mary, and Joseph.

We ask you Mary and Joseph to take us with all our hopes and desires. Please offer them with Jesus in the Holy Spirit to our heavenly Father, in union with each Mass offered throughout all time.

We consecrate ourselves to archangels Michael, Gabriel, and Raphael, and each angel, especially our guardian angel. We ask in the name of Jesus, through our Mother Mary, Queen of all Angels, that you, O heavenly Father, send forth legions of angels to minister to us:

Archangel Michael with his legions to ward off the attacks of the world, the flesh, and the devil;

Archangel Gabriel with his legions to teach us that we may know and do your will, and that they may help us to catechize and evangelize;

> *Archangel Raphael with his legions to heal our wound-*
> *edness, supply for our limitations, and strengthen us*
> *in our weakness to overcome demonic depression, to*
> *give us joy in the Spirit, to protect us in our travels*
> *and to supply all our needs.*
>
> *Finally, we ask for the gift of unconditional love, that we*
> *can live the love-life which was reflected in the holy*
> *family at Nazareth, thus bringing about justice and*
> *peace throughout the world. Amen.*

N

Novenas. Novenas are formal prayers said for nine days for a particular intention. It usually takes about ten minutes to say such a novena, which includes Scripture, reflections, and short prayers called aspirations.

One example of this devotion is the Pentecost novena (described in chapter five), which is usually said for the sanctification of one's own soul through the Holy Spirit. Or one can pray a novena for a special intention of a more specific nature, such as the healing of a sick relative.

In the Philippines, novenas play a large role in lay spirituality. Sometimes there are novenas in church, a different one on each day of the week. On Friday, the novena might be addressed to the Sacred Heart; on other days to the Filipino saint Lorenzo Ruiz, to Our Lady of Perpetual Help, to St. Martin de Porres, or to St. Joseph. These novenas last up to two hours and include various ceremonies.

O

Offering up. It is an old Catholic custom to offer to God as a sacrifice the annoyances and crosses of each day. These short prayers are usually expressed along these lines:

"I offer this pain for the souls in purgatory."
"I offer up this traffic jam for my son to get off drugs."
"Jesus, Mary, Joseph, I love you, save souls."

Short prayers of this kind, also called aspirations, help us to avoid giving in to irritation, discouragement, and despair. They also remind us that Jesus can unite our sufferings to his merits to use for the salvation of souls.

These prayers punctuate the day with a remembrance of God.

Using these short prayers can lead to a practice much loved in the Orthodox Church and adopted by the Western Church. This is the Jesus prayer, which consists in constantly praying the name of Jesus or the words, "Lord, Jesus Christ, have mercy on me, a poor sinner." Eventually the Jesus prayer can settle into the rhythm of one's breathing and enter into the heart in a way that is truly sanctifying.

Our Lady of Fatima suggests not only offering sufferings that come to us unbidden but also offering sacrifices, especially for the salvation of sinners (including oneself, of course!). Such sacrifices could consist in fasting, saying prayers, or undertaking unpleasant tasks that could have been avoided.

P

Papal blessing. You will find in some Catholic homes a beautifully colored and framed parchment inscribed with a blessing from the pope and with the names of family members. This can be hung on the wall near your prayer area or in any other place you think suitable.

You do not have to go to Rome for an audience to obtain this blessing. Write to Hardy Austin Associates, Dept. NCCR, 421 W. Union Ave, Bound Brook, NH 08805, or call 1-800-526-3939 to find out how to obtain such a blessing, signed and sealed by a papal delegate in Rome.

Papal picture. Many Catholic homes have a picture of the Holy Father on the wall to remind themselves of his authority and also that he stands in need of our daily prayers.

Pilgrimages. From earliest days, Catholics have found it a spiritual help to make pilgrimages to the Holy Land, to Rome, to famous shrines such as St. James of Compostela in Spain or Our Lady of Guadalupe in Mexico City, to Lourdes, Fatima, Knock, and other places. In olden times such pilgrimages were often assigned as penance for grave sins and involved enormous sacrifices such as walking barefoot for hundreds of miles. Nowadays, if you have the money it is easy to find relatively low-priced pilgrimages with accommodations that, if not luxurious, are comfortable (the emphasis being more on prayer than on severe penance).

Ardent Catholics can receive many graces toward

holiness from such pilgrimages; God, as it were, honors their sacrifice of time and effort with special gifts. Many conversions are reported as a result of pilgrimages by non-Catholics and also by lukewarm Catholics or ones who have fallen into serious sin. (Often these people may go on the pilgrimage at the urging of relatives and friends, and often at their expense.)

Praying for vocations, seminarians, priests, bishops, and the pope. Praying daily for vocations and for seminarians, priests, bishops, and the pope is the custom of many Catholics. (Some other Catholics, however, seem to spend more time criticizing priests, bishops, and the Holy Father than praying for them!)

Here is a prayer composed by the pope for vocations:

Lord, Jesus Christ, good Shepherd of our souls you know your sheep and know how to reach man's heart. Open the minds and hearts of those young people who search for and await a word of truth for their lives; let them understand that only in the mystery of your Incarnation do they find full light; arouse the courage of those who know where to seek the truth, but fear that what you ask would be too demanding, stir the hearts of those young people who would follow you, but who cannot overcome doubts and fears, and who in the end follow other voices and other paths which lead nowhere. You who are the Word of the Father, the Word which creates and saves, the Word which enlightens and sustains hearts, conquer with your Spirit the resistance and delays of indecisive hearts; arouse in those whom you call the courage of love's answer: "Here I am, send me!" (Is 6:8)

This beautiful prayer is based on the intercessory spirituality of Conchita. This Mexican grandmother, who is about to be beatified, founded many orders and pious associations dedicated to praying for priests:

O Jesus, I pray for your faithful and fervent priests; for your unfaithful and tepid priests; for your priests laboring at home, or abroad in distant mission fields; for your tempted priests; for your lonely and desolate priests; for your young priests; for your dying priests; for the souls of your priests in purgatory.

Above all, I recommend to you the priests dearest to me; the priest who baptized me; the priests who absolved me from my sins; the priests at whose Masses I assisted and who gave me your body and blood in Holy Communion; the priests who taught and instructed me; all the priests to whom I am indebted in any other way.

O Jesus, keep them all close to your heart, and bless them abundantly in time and in eternity. Amen.

A group of lay persons, who are connected to St. John's Seminary of the Archdiocese of Los Angeles and who pray for seminarians, collaborated on this prayer written by Lorraine de Necochea:

A Prayer for Seminarians

Father, God of love, send us your Son Jesus, the Good Shepherd, to lead us.

Help us. Renew our hearts to love Jesus and to serve you as we pray for our seminarian brothers whom you are calling forth as new shepherds.

Send forth your angels to minister to our seminarian brothers as they grow in your truth and in your love.

*Give them your wisdom, courage, and strength that they
will have no fear; give them a bold spirit and the
heart of the Good Shepherd.*

*Give them a pure desire to love all your children with
your unconditional love. By your Holy Spirit, guide
them to lean on you and on your Son Jesus in all
things.*

*Strengthen us all by the body and blood of Jesus; protect
us and sanctify us. Amen.*

Praying for the souls in purgatory. The most
famous, and also the shortest, prayers for this intention
are simply to say often during the day and night [1]
"Jesus, Mary, Joseph, I love you: save souls!" or *"Eternal
rest grant unto them, O Lord, and let perpetual light
shine upon them, and may they rest in peace."*

Praying for victims of disaster or violence. It is traditional for many Catholics to pray while traveling for
those who are victims of accidents. This practice teaches
children that a Christian's immediate response to ter-
rible events is to commend the victims to God's mercy
and blessing, rather than only to shudder with dread.

Some families also encourage praying for the victims
of calamities that are shown on TV or reported in the
newspapers.

Praying for one's children during the Mass. Some
mothers and fathers have the custom of praying for the
soul of each child as the priest raises the chalice during
the consecration. This symbolizes an inner release of
the child to Christ.

Praying over the suffering. Praying over members of the family and of the church community is a practice that became popular through the charismatic renewal. It consists in laying hands on the head, shoulders, or other part of the body that is in need of healing and praying aloud informally or in tongues for the intention requested.

This type of prayer can be effective with children, teens, young adults, and even lapsed Catholics, who may be "allergic" to more formal prayers. They are often especially willing to be prayed over when they are afraid—before bed, after a nightmare, when menaced by evil forces, or when threatened by sickness or death.

Processions. Especially in traditionally Catholic countries, there are frequent processions on feast days in honor of Jesus and Mary and other saints beloved by Catholics in that culture. These involve carrying banners and statues through the streets around the church, singing hymns and reciting litanies.

Prostration before the crucifix. Lying face down before a crucifix or picture of Jesus is an expression of adoration and submission to God. Prostration is most commonly practiced when alone, as a form of surrender to God's will.

In Ireland, there is usually a crucifix displayed prominently in the home. Years ago, devout souls would prostrate themselves before it as the Spirit moved them.

R

Relics. The custom of cherishing relics, like family heirlooms, is a long-standing one, mentioned in early Church history. Usually such mementos of the saints are handed down within religious orders or from friend to friend.

There are various types of relics. First-class relics are actual, tiny pieces of a saint's body, such as a bit of hair or bone; second-class relics are taken from garments the saint wore or objects he or she used; third-class relics are other objects, usually small pieces of cloth, that have been touched to a first-class relic. First-class relics are usually passed down with Vatican documents that certify their validity, insofar as this is possible.

The most prized relics are tiny splinters of the true cross of Jesus. Witty scoffers like to claim that these must be phony since, if you put them all together, they would make much more than one cross; however, some Catholic researchers have shown that these relics do in fact add up to about the size of a cross of the Roman era, which was a huge wooden object.

Some non-Catholics and also some Catholics think it is morbid to gather relics. They might consider analogies such as these: the way lovers often exchange a lock of hair; how lovers or best friends might prick their fingers and rub the blood together; how the bereaved cling to pieces of hair or clothing of their beloved dead. In the Victorian era, it was customary for women to wear lockets with such pieces of hair coiled within.

Retreats and days of recollection and workshops. It is a time-honored custom in the Catholic Church for lay people as well as religious to open themselves to greater closeness to God by setting aside special, longer times of prayer as frequently as once a year. These times of meditation, quiet prayer, and reflection—often guided by a retreat director—can help people to overcome chronic sinful patterns or to make important decisions.

Such periods of prayer might be half-days, whole days (sometimes called Days of Recollection), weekends, or longer periods ranging up to thirty days. Often Catholics use this time to attend spiritual workshops or retreats (usually announced in the diocesan newspaper).

In Russia, Catholics and Orthodox have a tradition of making a special kind of retreat called a *poustinia.* The retreatant goes off for a day or much longer to a somewhat isolated hut near a monastery for solitary prayer; food is supplied by a monk or a nun.

Poustinias have become known to Catholics in the United States through the work of Catherine de Hueck Doherty, who founded the Madonna House Apostolate in Canada. She emigrated to the West from Russia in the first part of this century and wrote a book, *Poustinia,* that describes the benefits of this Russian prayer in solitude. As a result of the popularity of this book, some monasteries offer lay people as well as religious the opportunity for truly isolated silent retreats on their grounds.

Many Catholics who may not be able to afford the time or the money involved in making longer retreats prefer to attend a Day of Recollection in the parish or at a nearby convent or retreat house. Or they might organize a bus trip to a nearby cathedral, monastery, or shrine.

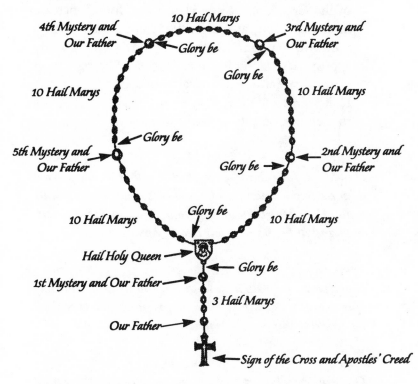

The Rosary. The rosary is a prayer that became popular in the Church at a time when many Catholics could not read the beautiful prayers of the Liturgy of the Hours. According to tradition, Our Lady revealed this prayer to St. Dominic and recommended it as a way for Catholics to ponder in their hearts the joyful, sorrowful, and glorious mysteries of the life of Jesus in an easy-to-understand form. For a complete listing of these mysteries, refer to a prayer book such as *The Catholic Prayer Book.*

The rosary recalls the principal mysteries of our salvation in groups of five decades (chaplets). Each group of five decades is preceded by the recitation of the Creed, and three Hail Marys for an increase in faith, hope, and charity. It concludes with a recitation of one of the anthems to Our Lady appropriate to the liturgical season. The repetition of the prayers of each decade, one Our Father, ten Hail Marys and one Glory be to the Father, helps us to meditate deeply on God's love for us.[8]

HAIL MARY

Hail Mary, full of grace, the Lord is with thee. Blessed art thou among women and blessed is the fruit of thy womb, Jesus. Holy Mary, Mother of God, pray for us, sinners, now and at the hour of our death. Amen.

GLORY BE

Glory be to the Father, and to the Son, and to the Holy Spirit. As it was in the beginning, is now, and ever shall be, world without end. Amen.

OUR FATHER

Our Father, who art in Heaven, hallowed be thy name. Thy kingdom come, thy will be done, on earth as it is in heaven. Give us this day our daily bread and forgive us our trespasses as we forgive those who trespass against us, and lead us not into temptation, but deliver us from evil. Amen.

HAIL, HOLY QUEEN

Hail! Holy Queen, Mother of Mercy, our life, our sweetness and our hope. To thee do we cry, poor banished children of Eve; to thee do we send up our sighs, mourning and weeping in this vale of tears. Turn then, O most gracious advocate, thine eyes of mercy toward us; and after this our exile, show unto us the blessed fruit of thy womb, Jesus. O clement, O loving, O sweet Virgin Mary! Pray for us, O Holy Mother of God, that we may be made worthy of the promises of Christ.

APOSTLES' CREED

I believe in God, the Father almighty, Creator of heaven and earth; and in Jesus Christ, his only Son, our Lord; who was conceived by the Holy Spirit, born of the Virgin Mary, suffered under Pontius Pilate, was crucified, died and was buried. On the third day, he rose again, in fulfillment of the Scriptures. From thence, he shall come to judge the living and the dead. I believe in the Holy Spirit, the holy Catholic Church, the communion of saints, the forgiveness of sins, the resurrection of the body, and life everlasting. Amen.

In deference to the wishes of Our Lady of Fatima many Catholics conclude each decade of the rosary with the words "O my Jesus, forgive us our sins, save us from the fires of hell, and lead all souls to heaven, especially those most in need of thy mercy."

Some Catholics prefer to pray the rosary by meditating on Scriptures appropriate to each decade, one for each bead. Suggestions for this can be found in a tiny book called *The Scriptural Rosary,* available in Catholic bookstores. This is especially helpful in introducing the rosary to non-Catholics to show how biblical it really is.

Many Catholics carry the rosary in their pockets or purses, wear a rosary ring, or keep a rosary under their pillow. This way it is handy for praying while driving, waiting in line, or trying to fall asleep. Sometimes Catholics say the rosary with others by buying a rosary tape for home or car, or (in cities where this is possible) by tuning in a TV or radio program where the rosary is said.

In the past it was much more common than it is now to find families praying the rosary every evening after dinner or before bed. Due to the messages of Mary at the alleged apparitions of Medjugorje, many Catholics who previously rarely said the rosary now say the fifteen decades in their own homes. Or they recite the rosary with other families in the parish by saying it in a different home each evening.

Some families like not only to recite the rosary but to make rosaries while they sit around in the evening.

S

The Sabbath. Observant Jews like to celebrate the Sabbath (Friday sundown to Saturday sundown) as has been done since earliest Old Testament times. This involves avoiding all menial labor and introducing the Sabbath with a special meal and prayers led by the mother. Although the practice varies according to whether Jews are Orthodox, Conservative, or Reform, in some families it is only the men who are obliged to go to the synagogue on Saturday morning for a formal service.

Some people who came into the Catholic faith from a Jewish background like to retain the Jewish Sabbath service in their families. This tradition can also help

Catholic families of non-Jewish backgrounds to under-stand the Jewish roots of Christian traditions, especially the Last Supper.

In honor of the Resurrection, Christians celebrate the first day of the week, rather than the seventh, as a day set aside for God. In former times almost all Catholic families made Sunday special: they avoided all work for pay, went to Mass together in the morning, and then had a large family meal followed by conversation and games. Now there is little sense of Sunday as a whole day of Sabbath rest. There are various reasons for this: changing work conditions that oblige many people to work on Sundays in order to survive financially, the option of a Saturday evening Mass, or the general dispersion of family members to separate activities.

Some families and some lay communities, especially charismatic covenant communities, have instituted a renewal of the tradition of a real celebration of the Lord's Day. Members gather for a prayer service which precedes an especially good dinner. These services vary in length; here is the text of one. Prior to the ceremony, the table should be provided with wine, a wine cup, bread, a candle, and matches.

THE LORD'S DAY CELEBRATION[9]

The Lighting of the Candle. The Assistant usually presides over the Lighting of the Candle. For a shortened form ceremony you may omit the passage from John 1:1-5.

Assistant: In the beginning was the Word and the Word was with God and the Word was God.

Group: All things were made through him and without him nothing was made that has been made.

A: In him was life and the life was the light of men.

G: The light shines in the darkness and the darkness has not overcome it. (Jn 1:1-5)

A: Heavenly Father, in honor of your Son, Light of the World and Author of Life, we are about to kindle the light for the Lord's Day. On this day you raised your Son Jesus from the dead and began the new creation. May our celebration of his resurrection this day be filled with your peace and heavenly blessing. Be gracious to us and cause your Holy Spirit to dwell more richly among us.

Father of Mercy, continue your loving kindness toward us. Make us worthy to walk in the way of your Son, loyal to your teaching and unwavering in love and service. Keep far from us all anxiety, darkness, and gloom; and grant that peace, light, and joy ever abide among us.

G: For in you is the fountain of life, in your light do we see light.

Light the candle and recite the following blessing:

A: Blessed are you, Lord our God, who created light on the first day and raised your Son, the Light of the World, to begin the new creation.

Blessed are you, Lord our God, King of the Universe, who give us joy as we kindle the light for the Lord's Day.

G: Amen.

For a short form of the ceremony, the following set of exhortations and responses are omitted:

Leader: Let us trust in the Lord and in his saving help.

Group: The Lord is my light and my salvation.

L: Let us receive his life and rejoice in his presence.

G: He is the true light that enlightens every man.

L: Let us keep his commandments and walk in his ways.

G: His word is a lamp to my feet and a light for my path.

L: Let us proclaim his goodness and show forth his glory.

G: We are the light of the world and the salt of the earth.

The Blessing of the Meal
and the Setting Aside of the Day

The Opening Proclamation. The following blessing is a proclamation to introduce the meal and normally would be said entirely by the leader but can also be read responsively, as indicated:

Leader: Brothers and sisters, this is the Lord's Day.

Group: Let us welcome it in joy and peace.

L: Today we set aside the concerns of the week that we may honor the Lord and celebrate his Resurrection. Today we cease from our work in order to worship God and remember the eternal life to which he has called us.

G: The Lord himself is with us, to refresh and strengthen us.

L: Let us welcome God among us and give him glory.

G: Let us love one another in Christ.

L: May the Holy Spirit be with us, to deepen our devotion to the Lord and to increase our zeal for the way of life he has given us.

It is possible to insert here a song or a time of praise.

THE BLESSING OF THE WINE.

Pour wine into the cup, raise it, and recite the following prayer:

Leader: Let us praise God with this symbol of joy and thank him for the blessings of the past week—for health, strength, and wisdom, for our life together in *(name of parish or family)*, for the discipline of our trials and temptations, for the happiness that has come to us out of our work.

THE SETTING ASIDE OF THE DAY.

This blessing welcomes the day and consecrates it to the celebration of the Lord's Resurrection:

Leader: Blessed are you, Lord our God, for the true rest you have given us in your Son Jesus and for this day which is a commemoration of his redeeming work. We welcome this day with gladness and consecrate it to the celebration of his Resurrection and of the new creation founded in him. Look graciously upon your servants and show us your glory. Blessed are you, Lord our God, who favor your people in the days set aside to your honor.

Group: Amen.

The Leader drinks from the cup and passes it to the others present.

THE BLESSING OF THE BREAD.

The Leader takes bread and recites the following blessing:

Leader: The eyes of all look to you, O Lord, and you give them their food in due season.

Group: You open your hand, you satisfy the desire of every living thing.

L: Blessed are you, Lord our God, King of the Universe, who bring forth bread from the earth.

G: Amen.

Distribute the bread and begin the meal.

A simple way to mark Sunday is to have your children tell you at Sunday dinner what the priest said in the sermon. One English priest I know attributes his own love of preaching to this practice of being trained to listen well in his youth.

Sometimes parents experience a good deal of stress just trying to keep their children quiet during the Mass—let alone helping them listen to the homily! The Vietnamese have found a solution. In Vietnam it is customary for all the children to sit around the altar or for the children to sit in the front pews with monitors; the adults sit behind them. Now in some parishes in the United States too, special attention is often given to the children at Mass. Sometimes, for example, there is one designated Sunday Mass where they are invited to sit around the altar.

In the Philippines, every Sunday is special—a time when the whole family gathers with the grandparents in the morning to eat special foods. The grandfather is in charge of leading prayer during the meal at lunch.

Scapulars. A scapular is a piece of cloth suspended over the shoulders by a string on the chest or on the chest and the back. Some monks and nuns wear long scapulars over their habits. However, going way back to early times of Church history, lay people have worn modified scapulars: these are usually one-inch squares of rough material of different colors and with special symbolic meanings.

Service and the apostolate. The life of many good Catholic Christians is a matter of twenty-four hour service to family, friends, neighbors, and society. This is especially true of those whose work itself involves serving others either in a direct Catholic lay ministry—in education or hospital work—or in work of any type that is geared primarily to increasing the common good.

Many Catholics choose to add other specific services to these basic works of love: befriending neglected young people, running Twelve-Step programs, helping once a week at the soup kitchen, collecting used goods for the poor, lectoring, being a Eucharistic minister, administering programs, hosting, speaking, writing, ministry in the arts, and so on.

There are many groups in the Church that Catholics can join to strengthen their joint witness.

The sign of the cross. Catholics make the sign of the cross, blessing themselves with or without holy water, by touching the middle fingers of the right hand to the forehead, the heart, and each shoulder, and saying

"In the name of the Father, and of the Son, and of the Holy Spirit. Amen."

The sign of the cross is made with holy water on

entering a church, but is also offered at other times as a tiny prayer renewing one's baptism and reaffirming one's identity as a Christian by invoking the blessing of the Holy Trinity. In Italian and Latino countries it is customary, after the sign of the cross, to bring one's fingers, pressed together, to the mouth.

Older Catholics like to make the sign of the cross when they pass a church to show their reverence for Jesus present in the tabernacle.

Stations of the Cross. These are pictures, plaques or statues representing the Passion of Jesus that hang in all churches— usually high on the walls surrounding the pews, or outdoors at retreat centers, or sometimes in a back yard or on a staircase in a Catholic home. Catholics traditionally pray the stations of the cross on Friday, especially Good Friday. Latino Catholics as well as Filipinos sometimes do penance or pray for others by praying the stations on their knees.

Some families make pictures of the stations to hang in the home or to mount on poles in the garden. If you are interested in doing this, you might visit a church where the stations are clearly labeled, study them, and then make your own set.[10]

Statues. In the early Church there was much discussion about whether holy statues violated the prohibition against idols. The Catholic use of statues is not designed to encourage worship, but is meant as an aid to remembering Jesus and the saints and cherishing them. Many Catholics buy beautiful statues of

Jesus, Mary, the Infant Jesus, and the saints to have in their homes and also near their front doors. Larger ones are sometimes arrayed on the front lawn, where they function not only to remind the family or community of the kingdom of God but also to witness to neighbors.

T

Thanksgiving. Catholics like to thank God frequently for blessings such as food and shelter, family and friends, and all the other good things of each day. Teaching children to do this helps to overcome the spirit of grumbling by the spirit of gratitude.

Third Orders and other apostolic groups. Most (though by no means all) very ardent Catholics feel called to unite with others in the pursuit of holiness of life. One way to do this is by joining a lay group that is affiliated to a religious order—the Third Orders of St. Benedict, St. Dominic, or St. Francis; Secular Carmelites; the Immaculata (of St. Maximilian Kolbe)—or by becoming an auxiliary of some other order.

The desire for a communal way of seeking holiness can also lead to joining a particular group not connected with a religious order: a charismatic covenant community, the Knights of Columbus, the Legion of Mary, Opus Dei, Cursillo, Communion and Liberation, or the Focolare.

V

Videos. Today a new custom is developing with the production of wonderful Catholic videos for children and for adults. Such videos are available in Catholic religious goods stores or through religious distribution catalogs.

Because children love videos, this is a good way for grandparents to reach out to their grandchildren if their own children are away from the Church for a time.

Visiting Christ at church. For many centuries it has been the custom for Catholics to "make a visit" to Jesus by stopping in at church for a short or long prayer. Some Catholic children are encouraged to make a visit every day on the way home from school.

W

Wearing a crucifix. Whereas many non-Catholic Christians wear a simple cross without the body of Christ on it, the Catholic tradition is to wear a cross that includes the body of the crucified Christ on it. This is a remembrance that he died for our sins and a way of showing that he is the center of our lives.

Weddings. Apart from the liturgy itself, many of the customs that Catholics follow for weddings are also part of the wider culture regardless of religious heritage. Brides wear white and grooms black; there are groomsmen and bridesmaids and traditions about them; people throw rice, and so on. One marriage custom that is particularly Catholic, however, is for the bride to offer her wedding bouquet to Mary at the foot of her statue in the church.

Slovakian Catholic weddings include some interesting customs. During the wedding Mass, a cross is placed on the altar; later the same cross is given to the couple, to be displayed prominently in their home. As the couple leaves the church after the Mass, they walk with the priest and hold a side of his stole; this symbolizes the unity of the Church and the couple. At the reception the bride's mother removes the bridal veil and replaces it with a scarf (babushka), a symbol of the bride's new state in life.

Writing letters to God. A custom that was begun as an exercise for retreatants in the seventies has caught hold and become part of the prayer life of some Catholics. The practice consists in writing a letter to God telling him how you feel about your life with all its problems. You then invoke the Holy Spirit and ask him to inspire you with a response that comes from God. Then you write down what you think God might be telling you about these problems.

Without pretending that such a method yields results that can be ascribed with complete certainty to God, people often find that such an endeavor is a new way to open them to truths they may not have focused on through their usual way of praying.

Afterword

When I started working on *The Book of Catholic Customs and Traditions*, I knew I would enjoy passing on to others the customs I had loved as a child. Now, as a result of our research, I have found many new and fascinating customs and traditions to pass on to my own family. I hope that you will enjoy these customs and traditions as much as we do.

Carla Chervin Conley

Carla Chervin Conley

Notes

THREE
The Christmas Season

1. David Cawkwell, *At Home with the Word 1994* (Chicago: Liturgy Training Publications, 1994), 39.
2. George Peate, taken from a prayer card produced by Third Millenium Publications, P.O. Box 1126, Thousand Oaks, CA 91360. Used by permission.

FOUR
The Lenten Season

1. For more information, write to Catholic Relief Services, USCC, P.O. Box 17220, Baltimore, MD 21298-9663.
2. The Lord's Day celebration book mentioned in chapter seven contains one such Passover service.
3. Hebrew-Catholic Association, Box 798, Highland, NY 12528.

FIVE
The Easter Season

1. Anthony Bullen, ed., *A Liturgical Prayer Book* (Ann Arbor, Mich.: Servant, 1991), 42. To obtain a booklet with all the prayers and reflections for this novena, write to Merciful Love, P.O. Box 24, Fresno, CA 93707.
2. Bullen, 42.
3. To find out about arranging your own Eucharistic home shrine write to Mrs. Marion P. Barnwell, 1207 East Maple Avenue, El Segundo, CA 90245.

SIX
Ordinary Time

1. St. Louis Marie de Montfort, *True Devotion to Mary* (Bay Shore, N.Y.: Montfort Publications, 1941), 228.
2. Bullen, 36.
3. Used by permission of Sister Marsaia Kaster.
4. You can read more about Kateri in the book *Adventures with a Saint: Kateri Tekakwitha: Lily of the Mohawks,* by Marlene McCauley (Phoenix: Grace House Publishing Co., 1992).
5. *The Catholic Prayer Book,* compiled by Monsignor Michael Buckley (Ann Arbor, Mich.: Servant, 1986), 235.
6. *Following Christ,* Book 6 of "Faith and Life Series" (San Francisco: Ignatius Press, 1985), 139.
7. Omer Englebert, *St. Francis of Assisi* (Ann Arbor, Mich.: Servant, 1979), 251.
8. You can get a catalog by calling (805) 944-1047, or write to St. Andrew's Abbey, Valyermo, CA 93563.
9. For more information, write to The Central Association of the Miraculous Medal, 475 E. Chelten Ave., Philadelphia, PA 19144.
10. A beautiful little booklet containing these prayers can be obtained from Maryhurst Press, 1223 Maryhurst Drive, St. Louis, MO 63122.
11. To find out about arranging your own Eucharistic home shrine, write to Mrs. Marion Barnwell, 1207 East Maple Avenue, El Segundo, CA 90245.

SEVEN
Customs and Traditions for the Whole Year

1. *The Catholic Prayer Book,* 236.
2. Frances Larkin, SS.CC., *Understanding the Heart* (San Francisco: Ignatius, 1975), 121-22. Used by permission.
3. From prayer card produced by Missionaries of the Eternal Word, P.O. Box 1799 Largo, FL 33540-0135. Imprimatur: Manuel, Bishop of Barcelona, Dec. 19, 1931.
4. Bullen, 149.
5. *The Catholic Prayer Book,* 103.
6. Bullen, 50.
7. The Mystical Mass Prayer can be ordered as an attractive prayer leaflet from The Christian Renewal Center, 411 First St., Fillmore, CA 93015. Used by permission.
8. *The Catholic Prayer Book,* 245.
9. Servant Ministries, *Celebrating the Lord's Day* (Ann Arbor: Servant, 1986). Throughout this ceremony, the "Leader" is the head of the household, most commonly the father of the family. "Assistant" is either

the person next in authority or next eldest to the Leader, most commonly the mother of the family. "Group" is all the household members and any guests who may be present. When the letters "G," "A," and "L" appear in parentheses, it indicates that the reading may be done responsively as marked, if more group participation is desired.

10. You can obtain the beautiful traditional prayers for the stations of the cross from any religious goods store. You can also order a tape of the stations from the Knights of Columbus, P.O. Box 68, Plattsburgh, NY 12901.

Index

Another Book of Interest to Servant Readers

Prayers of the Women Mystics
Ronda De Sola Chervin

"Praise to you, Spirit of Fire! to you who send the timbrel and lyre. Your music sets our mind ablaze. The strength of our souls awaits your coming in the tent of meeting." —Hildegard of Bingen

This lyrical and imaginative prayer invoking the Holy Spirit was penned by a famous medieval mystic and is but a sample of the many stirring prayers in this collection. Journey in prayer with great women mystics and through the prism of mystical prayer, glimpse their profound intimacy with God. Gertrude the Great, Birgitta of Sweden, Julian of Norwich, Catherine of Siena, Teresa of Avila, and fourteen other mystics are included.

Each chapter on a particular mystic includes commentary on her life and spirituality and a selection of prayers organized by key themes. *Prayers of the Women Mystics* will appeal to all Christians who desire deeper intimacy with God, especially those attracted to mystical experience and prayer. *$7.99*